The Ultimate

Fish Story

Harry Haney

Illustrated by

Gillian Bradshaw-Smith

The Ultimate Fish Story

Harry Haney

*Illustrated by
Gillian Bradshaw-Smith*

✝ Divine Mercy Press ✝

Dallas, Texas/Oceanside, California

Without limiting the rights under copyright reserved above, no part of this publication may be reproduced, stored in or introduced into a retrieval system, or transmitted, in any form or any means (electronic, mechanical, photocopying, recording, or otherwise), without the prior written permission of the copyright owner.

Please Note: This book is a memoir of fishing stories. Although the author endeavored to insure the accuracy of these memories, some allowance must be made for human error.

Every effort made to contact other persons mentioned in these stories for required permissions. If you feel you are portrayed in one of these stories, please contact the author at www.theultimatefishstory.com.

The theological ideas expressed herein are not necessarily those of Divine Mercy Press or its staff.

Cover art and illustrations by Gillian Bradshaw-Smith
©2010 by Harry Eugene Haney Jr. and Gillian Bradshaw-Smith
Back cover photo by Harry Haney

1. Cataloging in Publication data
2. Haney, Harry Eugene
3. *The Ultimate Fish Story*, By Harry Haney
4. p. cm.
5. ISBN 9780975547120

First Printing June 2010

✠ Divine Mercy Press ✠

3216 Mission Avenue, Suite 138, Oceanside, California, 92058
5319 Willis Avenue, Dallas, Texas 75206

divinemercy@hypersurf.com

Table Of Contents

Opening My Stories	9
The Concrete Ship	13
Capitola Kayakers	19
Our First Trip	23
Getting Out In Bigger Waves	29
The First Big Wave Crash	33
The Physics Of It All	39
Learning To Fish In the Kelp	45
The Shark	51
Potty Break	57
The Lone Hunter	61
The Cliff Trail	65
Making Scallops	71
Whip Shot	77

Who's Got Who	83
Mean Green	89
The Price Of Fame	97
The Kids	103
The Painting	109
Raining Trout	113
Valerie's Balancing Act	119
Kowa's Canoe Training	125
Dad's Day	133
The Winter Storms	145
Walking on Water	149
Craig's Trip and the Ultimate Fish Story	159

8 | The Ultimate Fish Story

Opening My Stories

If you're an avid fisherman for very long, you've collected your share of outrageous and implausible fish stories. And anywhere two or more of you get together, you're always willing to swap your best stories to see whose wins. As fish stories go, there are some that stand out, and then, there's the one on top of the list. It's the one you always remember. The one you can use to win the current contest of the best fish story. Well, here are some of mine that have won countless contests and the one that has never been defeated.

Here's a collection of my personal experiences, leading up to what I've come to consider The Ultimate Fish Story. If Samuel Clemens could read this collection I know he'd get a chuckle.

So try to imagine the smell of salt air, mixed with decaying kelp carried on a chilly, damp fog. You'd be hearing and feeling the soft rumble of the surf in the background. The cry of a handful of sea gulls you can't see, but you know are somewhere close by, but obscured in the fog. You lean back against the sea wall, wiggle back and forth in the sand to make yourself a perfect copy of your backside and get comfortable. The fog is just starting to rise off the sand and water, like a curtain going up. You're looking out under the rising layer of fog at the endless blue horizon, that's where the stories happen, out there, on Mother Ocean.

The Concrete Ship

I lived on the Pacific coast of northern California, in the ever-so-small beach community of Aptos, lovingly called by the locals, "fogtos". This little micro- climate area maintained fog when no other local area of the coast could. If you take a look at a map of Monterey Bay, you'll find it's in the geographical center of the bay. I had a little house on the cliff overlooking the beach, in that lovely little community.

The view was a beautiful panorama of this side of the bay, a long crescent of shoreline disappearing into the ocean haze. Breaking up that perfect curve of the coastline and jutting out into the bay some five hundred feet was our pier and the "concrete ship". The pier with the USS PALO ALTO attached to the end of it was half a mile from my door. It was the favorite place for local fishermen and retired folks to go hang out, swap stories, and catch up on all the gossip of our little community. It was a place for people to walk to and back from, while remembering their youth. Built in the nineteen-twenties as a casino and dance joint, many of the old timers could tell you about going gambling or dancing back in the day. There had been a horse-drawn trolley from Santa Cruz down along the beach cliffs. Visitors were treated to a beautiful view of Monterey Bay. People would ride the trolley down, spend the evening at the casino, and ride the trolley back when they were through. But time and the sea had battered the old girl over the years. The fierce winter storms had swept away the entire wooden superstructure. The building that had been the casino was gone and her back had been broken in two places. The ship, *per se*, was closed to the public at the time I moved into the neighborhood. But I would have a major role in remedying that situation. The old timers would tell you of catching huge numbers of fish in the old days, just out there beyond the fence, and I, for one, wanted to have that happen again.

    Living in a beach community makes you one of the locals instantly. Anyone who can afford to own a house on the beach is given at least the chance to become a local. As I was introduced to the locals, they all talked of repairing the pier and restoring and reopening the old Palo Alto. One day, Rose Costa, the Godmother of the pier, asked if I'd be willing to help with the labor of restoring and reopening the pier. She said there were lots of volunteers but she needed someone to be in charge of the complete effort, someone who could go talk to the State Parks people about the legal stuff, and be responsible for scheduling deliveries of equipment and material. She would raise the money necessary to repair and reopen the ship. There were twenty or so real regulars, who during the course of the week would make at least one trip down to the pier to fish or gab. By the time we were ready to start work we had sixty-five volunteers signed up and liability releases from the state signed. After almost a year of work the pier reopened along with the boat. The State Parks Department brought the pomp and ceremony, and the fishing commenced off the old girl for the first time in fifteen years.

The problem was, only during the salmon, halibut, and rubber-lipped perch season were there any fish there. The rest of the time "it" was mostly drinking beer and socializing. I, on the other hand, was always looking for a new place to fish. I'd rather be fishing than just about anything else there is to do! In this one area of the coast there are three piers to chose from, the mile-long Santa Cruz Pier, The Capitola Pier and the concrete ship pier. The Capitola Pier was just up the coast road, so I decided to try fishing off it.

Capitola Kayakers

One day while I was fishing on the Capitola Pier (and not catching anything, by the way), I saw three guys at the beach with ocean-going kayaks. They had set their kayaks on the sand and were loading up to paddle out through the surf and into the bay. They all had wetsuits on, so I knew they were ready to get wet. I watched them navigate through the surf. They stood in about a foot of water holding their kayaks as the wave pushed in. When the wave was at full they hopped in, set down and started paddling. The wave washed out and took them along with it to meet the incoming wave. It looked like they were having fun. The three of them headed down the coast aways and then came back an hour or so later. They were out getting exercise and fresh air. I watched them negotiate the surf on their way back in. They had a steerable rudder on the rear to help keep them straight in the wave. Two of them made it; the other one was caught, turned sideways, and rolled over and over. He was summarily dumped out and washed up on the sand.

    This gave me a great idea. Valerie and I could do that with our canoe. My wife and I were training for an upcoming month-long canoe trip. We were planning to cross half of Canada, going down the Fraser River by canoe. It looked like it might be fun to add the rigor of going out through the surf to our régime. So we waited for a day when the surf was almost nonexistent. We loaded up and brought the canoe down to the beach to try it. There's something exciting about being at a beach, even more so when you're in the water. I think it brings out the kid in all of us and definitely adds to the adrenaline levels of the participants.

Our First Trip

Well, the canoe sat three feet from the water's edge, while we took off our shoes and socks. They got stashed into the ends of the canoe, as the temperature was a bit chilly. The paddles were also placed where we could easily get to them. The way out secmed easy as we both were experienced white water canoeists. I was a long-time surfer and well acquainted with the goings and comings of the surf. We waited for the little wave to wash out, walked out behind it, set the canoe down and Val jumped in and sat down. The little wave came back in and picked up the canoe. I took two little steps into the water and the third into the canoe. Mother Nature did the rest. As the wave receded it took us with it;

we were off. There we were, paddling out in the ocean on a gentle swell, with the smell of the cool salt air—just remembering gives me goose bumps.

The sky is so blue and the air so clean, only on the Pacific Coast can you find conditions like these. The wind blows across the entire Pacific Ocean, all the way from Japan, only tiny little Hawaii to add any pollution, and all that ocean to clean the air. I've lived there for twenty seven years. In my opinion, this had to have been the Garden of Eden, before the white man ruined it. The tribes of Indians that lived there for tens of thousands of years left behind three artifacts that have been found. It's a fact; the Monterey Bay area at one time had the greatest concentration of life on our planet.

We paddled around for an hour or so, before we decided it was time to head in. The gentle swell made almost no surf, but enough to pick up the fourteen foot canoe and push it silently toward the sand. It's like a big hand scoops you up and starts pushing you at the beach. This is the ground, folks: if you make it all the way in, you're going to hit that beach at fifteen to twenty miles an hour. . . But, not to worry, as the water gets shallower and before you come to an abrupt stop, you start to slide through the sand. This, by the way, is just about as smooth a break as you can find. Surfing in a canoe, with two people in it, was definitely an adrenaline rush.

Having been a surfer, sailor, commercial fisherman, and general all-round physics guy, I guided the rear end of the canoe and kept it riding the wave like a surf board right up onto the sand. When the water from the wave went back out, Val and I just stepped out of the canoe onto the sand. We each grabbed a side of the canoe. We took a couple of steps toward dry ground and set the canoe down, so the swell wouldn't pick it up again. Val came around and we plopped down in the warm sand to ponder our accomplishment. We were both excited. We had done it. This was our first of many adventures involving canoe and surf.

We were back the next day. The swell was up to a foot and a half which gave us three-foot wave fronts to practice on. Getting out wasn't all that difficult, although we did get some water over the nose of the canoe when it punched into the first three-foot wave. But we were up and over it racing to beat the next wave forming. We had to get to it before it broke and became a wall of foam. This was exciting, exhilarating, and soon to be dangerous; our kind of adventure.

Well, we were out for a while, resting, trying to get up the nerve to attempt going back in. We eased up to the surf line and watched the swell going underneath us. It was breaking right at the bow of the canoe. We sat through four waves; finally it was time to go. We let the wave break, and started paddling in behind it; so far, so good. But the wave behind us had broken and when it hit us we were picked up and pushed forward. It also pushed the nose of the canoe down and made us swing sideways, then roll. We had flipped the canoe for the first time and found out what it was like in the cold churning ocean. We needed to improve our canoeing skills and this was exactly how: Practice.

I built a domed nose cover over the first three-and-a-half feet, raised eight inches in the middle to punch through the waves. This kept a good deal of water out, and allowed us more daring attempts at larger waves.

Getting Out In Bigger Waves

Val and I sat there on the sand, watching the waves pounding the beach, the salt spray so thick in the air you could taste it, if you stuck out your tongue. The ground vibrated and the roar of crashing ten-foot waves made it difficult to hear each other, even a few feet away. Finally we steeled our nerves, grabbed the canoe and walked out into the churning foam, standing there in the rushing water holding the canoe, and waiting. Timing in the surf is everything and knowing what's outside, coming up next is crucial. I had made our choice, we couldn't wait.

"O.K., let's go", I yelled. Val got in, and started paddling. I pushed until I was afraid I couldn't get in the canoe. The front of the canoe was already rising on the wave when I jumped in, grabbed my paddle and pulled for all I was worth. The canoe was almost vertical; Val literally grabbed the green water on the crest of the wave with her paddle and pulled us over the top. Pulling together as hard as we could, we started into the next wave. We were a little farther into the second, the canoe punched through the top three feet. We didn't get nearly as vertical going over it and the third one was almost unexciting.

If you are wondering why we did this, we're a couple of adrenaline junkies. This was putting our life on the line for excitement, against being drowned. This was turning the wick up to maximum.

Getting out there was only the first part, and usually easier than getting back. Getting back was dangerous when the swell and waves were big. It took impeccable timing and perfect coordination between the front and the rear paddlers, and balance between us, all rolled into one.

32 _____ _The Ultimate Fish Story_

The First Big Wave Crash

We'd made it out through our first big waves and our adrenaline level was maxed. All the time we sat out there fishing, and not catching anything, I secretly worried about getting back through those six-foot waves. After a couple of hours with no fish we'd had enough and were ready to attempt getting back. We eased up the surf line and studied it very carefully. We were looking to see if we could catch a small set of waves to get in on. Unfortunately, they were all the same today. Eight identical waves and two larger ones and the set started over. We had decided the next two big waves and we'd go.

Here they came; as the second one reached us we started paddling toward the shore. I wanted to be as far in as I could get without catching the last big wave. This would put us as far ahead of the following (hopefully smaller wave) as possible. It did exactly that, but as I looked back over my shoulder at the oncoming wave, we had gotten too far ahead of it. It was going to break before it got to us. A white wall of churning water, six feet high, hit us from the rear. It covered me and launched the canoe forward and sideways at the same time. I heard Val scream "Oh my God" as we went over in front of the wall of foam. We were both dumped out, along with everything in the canoe, as the wall of foam flipped us over and over. We were trying to swim with our clothes on, while being tumbled in the foam and pushed by the wave behind it. It's like being caught in a giant washing-machine. There is a real danger in the white water of a wave. It's foam, you can't breathe in it and you can't swim in it. You can actually drown in the foam of a big wave. Surfers learn to duck back into the wave and swim down to get out of it. But this was Val's first time being caught in the foam. We tumbled end over end while trying to contain our fishing equipment and not get hit by the canoe being slammed over and over on top of us. I got hit twice by the canoe before I got a hold of it with a death grip, then it and I rolled together. About half drowned, we were trying to grab fishing poles, tackle box, the cooler, and the paddles all at the same time. I was so glad when we got in far enough that we could touch the bottom. At least now we didn't have to worry about drowning, just finding all our stuff. Valarie had the poles and cooler. It turned out that the cooler made a fairly nice life preserver. I had both paddles and the canoe. I could see the tackle box washed up on the sand thirty feet down the beach. Several hundred people playing around on the beach had stopped to watch the five-minute event. There we sat gasping for air. Soaked, looking like two very nearly drowned rats. Finally I got up and rolled the canoe over to dump out the water and sand. Then I drugged it up to dry ground and sat down again leaning against the canoe. Valarie got up and staggered over to pick up the tackle box. She turned it sideways on the way back and poured out the water. Then she plopped down next to me against the canoe; we both broke up laughing. The sun was warming us up as we were both shivering and quite blue from the cold.

There were a lot of crashes to spread our fame. Mainly because the beaches are hardly ever empty. You just didn't see anyone else trying to take a canoe in and out through the surf to go fishing. The ocean water in Santa Cruz is for the most part fifty-three degrees cold, year round. Our first crash into the beach was not our most spectacular by far.

But, we quickly learned what needed to be done with the equipment in the canoe, after trying to grab floating tackle boxes, cooler, fishing poles and the canoe while we were being tumbled in the white water of the wave. We came to the conclusion that everything in the canoe must be tied down, when coming in through any swell, other than on a flat day.

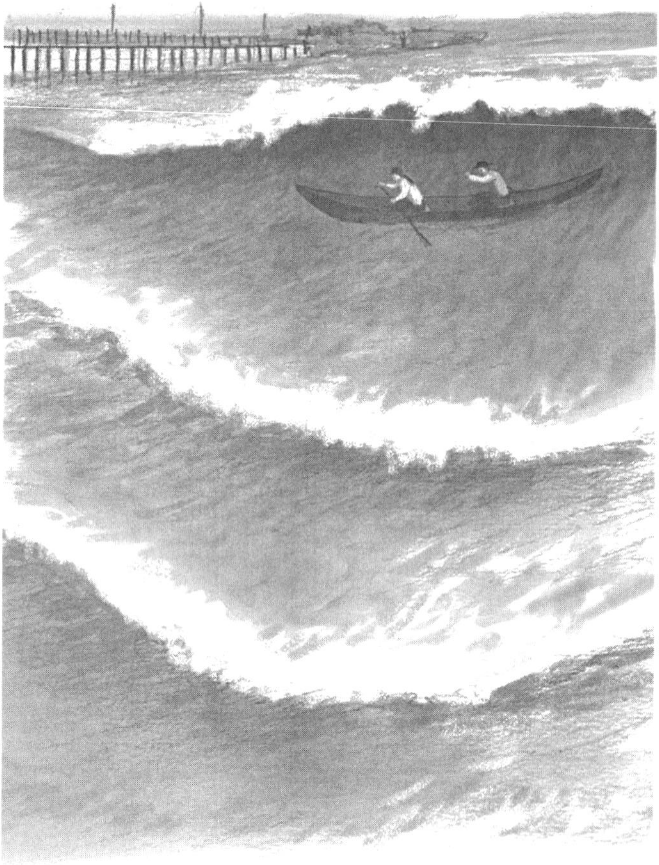

The Physics of It All

Our canoe was a fourteen-foot white water model. With two people in it, it sticks out of the water about eight inches in the middle and fourteen in the front and back. It's twenty-eight inches wide amid ship and made of ABS plastic; virtually indestructible. Now, put us in the canoe and add our height. About a meter on top of the seat, roughly, and you can see, most of the waves were over our heads.

The size of the wave front is twice the height of the swell. So, two-foot swell equals a four-foot wave, the average swell in Santa Cruz is a foot-and-a-half which makes a three-foot wave. The water is actually being pulled back out in front of the wall which makes it lower, but that's where they measure the height of the wave from. So a three foot wave doesn't stick up three feet from the back. You only see the swell looking at it from the back; but we were looking at them from the front.

O.K. Here we go! Take a two-foot swell, roughly moving twenty miles an hour. It's coming up behind the canoe. It begins to lift the rear end and push the canoe out in front of it. It's just like a surf board without a fin on it to keep it going straight. The person in the rear is responsible for driving the canoe and keeping it surfing in a straight line, while the bow man must anticipate which side is slipping out of the groove? They must "block" their paddle against the side of the canoe to give the stern guy something to drive against. If the bow person is proficient, very little is said and Valarie was an expert. If necessary the commands are simple: "left", "right", or maybe, "ease up a little".

Well, if you ever surfed, you know you can't go straight in. You have to angle across the wave, staying in the pocket. If you get too far in front of it, you start to slow down and it will run over you. If you get too far up in the wave it passes underneath you and leaves you to deal with the next wave coming right behind.

Sound difficult? It is, extremely difficult, which is, after all, why we became famous up and down the Monterey coast.

You with me so far? Good. . . On a surf board, the surfer can move front to rear depending on what the rider needs the board to do. Move forward, it goes faster, move back, it slows down. He can also drag his hand in the water to slow down. This is done relative to your position on the wave, not so in a canoe. If you let the nose get off to one side or the other it wants to slide sideways and then roll rather than surf on the wave because there's no fin on the bottom of the canoe as there is on a surfboard to keep it going in a straight line. Here's what I would see when the canoe rolled in the surf. It would start getting out of the pocket, sliding around sideways on the wave.

Sometimes, we could get it back straight, if I could cross-paddle with the bow person fast enough. But, if we couldn't, we had a split second to take a deep breath, because we knew we were going over face first into that icy water. The canoe was going to tumble over and over in the white water being pushed by the wave, until everything made its way to the beach.

We did that several times in quick succession before we learned how to balance front to rear. The front seat was positioned to balance the load of two people on flat water. When the wave started to push the canoe, it pushed the nose down into the water making more drag and impossible to steer. We needed more weight in the rear. So on our first try at rebalancing, Val moved back to amidships and sat on the cooler which had gotten tied to the cross thwart. This got the nose up and let the canoe be pushed out in front of the wave. Now, we could use our paddles to adjust the drag the canoe had going through the water. Like the surfer dragging his hand in the wave to slow down. It let us slow down as needed to stay in the groove. We waited for the next wave to begin picking up the back of the canoe and with a stroke of our paddles we were off, sliding toward the beach on the face of the wave. The adrenalin rush climbing as we're sped toward the sand of the beach. We made a perfect landing and when the water from the wave receded we just stepped out, picked up the canoe, and carried it a few feet past the water line.

44   *The Ultimate Fish Story*

Learning To Fish In the Kelp

Val and I were used to fly fishing for trout out of the canoe. We fished in our local area lakes, and an assortment of other lakes all the way to Canada and back. We had also been fly fishing locally for steel head salmon in the San Lorenzo River which ran from the town of Boulder Creek in the Santa Cruz Mountains down to Santa Cruz and the ocean. At the beach we used long surf rods, eight or nine feet, unsuitable for the canoe.

We decided we couldn't use our fly rods and the long surf rods were out, which left our small bait poles. They were small spinning rods we used to gig live bait on the Concrete Ship Pier. They were set up with four-pound test. So, the first time we took our fishing-poles out in the canoe, we didn't catch a thing. That's not to say we didn't have something bite. Every time a fish got on, two things happened, the end of the pole bent into the water and the line snapped.

We paddled back over to the pier, tied up the canoe next to the landing ladder, and climbed up. There was a bait and tackle shop there. I got us some ten pound test line to re-spool our reels. The guy working there was all questions, had we caught anything, what we were fishing for, etc. . . . Val and I sat on the edge of the pier, while we re-spooled our reels with the heavier line.

Afterward we paddled back out to the kelp bed, got tied up and started fishing again. We actually managed to catch what was down there. A half pound Gopher cod was our first fish out of the kelp bed. We still couldn't keep the end of the little poles out of the water or the line breaking. We managed to catch one out of five fish that we hooked. This was great fishing, every time we dropped our line in we had something take the bait. There seemed to be a huge number of fish to be had out here in the kelp bed and we aimed to get them. We just needed to get the right gear.

By the end of our outing we had decided a shopping trip was in order. We needed some short stout poles with reels that could hold heavy line and crank up big fish: we had high hopes. The nylon leaders we were using soon gave way to stainless steel and the reels wound up with eighty pound Dacron. We were ready to be *BIG FISH HUNTERS* and so we painted it on the side of the canoe.

Fishing in the kelp there's only twenty to sixty feet of water. The kelp has to anchor itself to the bottom and sixty feet is about its limit. So vertically, you only need that much line on your reel. However, in the other direction it requires a good deal of skill to keep your prey from tangling up in the kelp and getting away.

The new gear did the trick. Starting off with a pound-and-a-half gopher cod, then; two- three- and five-pounders were adorning our stringers. Several successful fishing excursions and our friends Kathy and Ralph, who had a two-place kayak, started going with us.

We had gotten the basics down and our fame had started to spread. There were several reasons why, the main one, though, was that we went in and out next to the Capitola Pier, a pier which always had people on it, as did the beach area on both sides. The people on the pier were fishing, "sort of", most of the time. You didn't generally catch anything from the pier. So they got used to seeing us go out and come back with stringers of fish, every time we went; sometimes several stringers. If you want to get a fisherman's attention, just walk by him with fish, when he hasn't caught any. People would meet us at the road to question us on how and where we caught all these fish. We'd laugh and say "Right over there" pointing to the kelp bed.

This got to be a regular sport. Fighting our way out through the surf, fishing, and making it back "dry" was the key. We didn't always get back completely dry. But we were daring and each trip added to our confidence. I'm not so sure now that it was a good thing. With our growing confidence, we would brave larger and larger waves. We were truly famous for taking our canoe out through the big surf.

50   *The Ultimate Fish Story*

The Shark

One day all four of us were out enjoying ourselves, catching fish left and right. Ralph had this metal stringer that had clips on it, that kept the fish separated by just a little. I think it held ten fish. We had caught more that that apiece. Val and I used heavy nylon line with a metal ring in the end of it and a pointed metal piece on the other. This went through the fish's gills, to keep from having to stick our fingers where you really didn't want them to be in the first place. These fish had real big nasty teeth that you had to stay away from. Valarie was keeping her stringer of fish tied to the seat with the fish dangling out past the end of the canoe; mine was likewise tied to my seat. Dragging those fish through the water became a problem when we would move to a new location. They would get tangled in the kelp. So we would boat the stringers of fish if we moved very far. We liked to stay close to Kathy and Ralph. We'd all be singing and carrying on out there where nobody else could hear, in case we added some politically incorrect words to our version of whatever we were singing. They called their kayak "The Fat Bottom Girl". Ralph loved that song, the more tequila he drank the louder he sang it.

Fishing had slowed down so we had decided to move out to the farthest kelp bed and into deeper water. So we boated our fish and headed out. When we got there, we would throw the fish back over the side. We tied up to the kelp and started fishing. Val and I were just getting our lines back in the water when the canoe was yanked completely around one hundred and eighty degrees. The sudden spin unbalanced us and nearly pulled us over; we just managed to keep from capsizing the canoe. We were both looking at each other in total amazement as we started looking around at our stuff. Everything looked O.K. at first, like it had before we had gotten spun around. The stringers hanging off the ends were still there, although several times they had come untied from the seat and the fish just swam away. Not this time, they were stilled tied in place.

Oh well, another one for the book. I guess I knew then that someday I'd have to put all of our adventures into a story and this would be one of them.

Several minutes later I caught another fish and went to untie my stringer. I pulled it up, no fish, and no stringer. "What the heck? Look at this, you guys! What do you make of this, Ralph?" I held up the frayed end of the line so everyone could see it.

"Big Shark" was all Ralph said and started laughing. "Can't think we're the biggest things out here, now, can you?" He was quite right. I knew from firsthand experience while scuba diving off Catalina Island. I've been face to face with a seven-foot blue shark and I knew I was not the biggest thing in this pond.

That summer the four of us made Saturday our "adventures at the beach" day. It was better than any ride at Disneyland because you could never tell what was going to happen, either on the trip out or the trip in. We had a ball, getting caught in a wave and rolled sideways or dumped out all together and having to chase the canoe or kayak as the case might be. Experience is a great teacher and if you want to get good at something, just go out and do it over and over, each time trying to add to your bag of tricks.

56 *The Ultimate Fish Story*

Potty Break

Spending the day out on the ocean fishing and drinking various liquors sounds like a great day. But eventually there comes the time you just can't stand it anymore and are forced to find a way to relieve yourself. We couldn't just run back onto the beach and use the facilities; when we went in we were in for the day. But depending on where we were and how far it was back to the pier we could go tie up and climb the ladder up, they had restrooms on the pier. But that could take a great deal of time especially if we had paddled two or more miles up the coast, which we did regularly. So we had to develop various balancing acts to accommodate the potty break. For the guys it wasn't too difficult. Get on your knees, balance the canoe, and take care of business. Still, it was much harder to balance the canoe when you're on your knees than sitting comfortably in the seat.

The girls really had it tough, but necessity will force you to find a way and they both came up with one. Seems it was easier for Val in the canoe than Kathy in the kayak. In the canoe you sat up five inches off the floor which allowed for a container under the seat; in the kayak, you sat on the floor. But Kathy was no slouch and found her own way to accomplish the task.

Now, do you think we would reel up our fishing line while we were indisposed in such a manner? Why heck NO! I would stick the pole under the seat so it couldn't be jerked over the side in case something got on it while I was busy. In fact, I use to say to the world at large "OK here's your big chance" and I can't count how many times that pole slammed into the water while I was balancing on my knees. It demanded stopping what I was doing right in the middle of it, grabbing the pole and catching the fish before finishing personal business. Is this dedication to catching fish possible? NO, it was self preservation as those short, stout, boat poles didn't bend easily into the water which gave the fish leverage to capsize the canoe. If the fish was really big it was hard to get the pole out from under the seat, as the fish had three-and-a-half foot leverage pulling down against me pulling back with the six inch handle of the pole. On several occasions the rail of the canoe made it into the water before I could get the pole lose; always adding to the adrenaline factor of being a *BIG FISH HUNTER*.

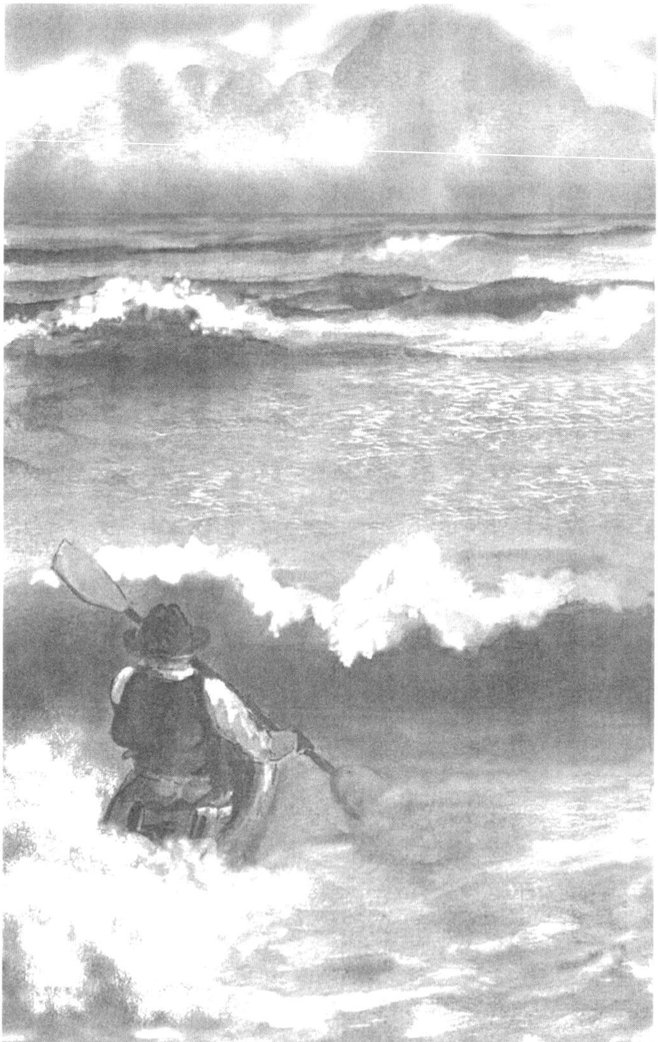

The Lone Hunter

As the summer passed and the winter weather moved in, it became more difficult to go out fishing, but any time the surf would allow, we'd go. After a while, Valerie got tired of going and I started going out by myself. I could carry everything by myself; it just took me more trips from the land cruiser to the beach. I'd go out on the incoming tide and back on the outgoing one. So I'd be out there for three or four hours most of the time. There were those times where I'd spent most of the day fishing, in between jobs for Intel.

We had developed the technique of dropping our line down next to giant kelp fronds coming up from the bottom. If you didn't get a bite by the time it got to the bottom you moved ten or so feet and tried again. Sometimes just on the other side of the kelp frond was enough to trigger a fish to bite. We liked to come back with ten fish or more. This was enough for us plus some to take down to the beach for our extended family. We would cover the entire area of one kelp bed hunting our quarry. If we met with no success, we'd paddle off to the next kelp bed to try our luck there. It seems these fish are very territorial and the biggest gets the prime location. We had been known to catch four or five fish at one stop. The first was generally the biggest but not always. Often the commotion of something flailing around would draw the nearby fish to investigate, at which point we were more than willing to add them to our collection.   There were a lot of small fish we'd throw back and we never kept the first one either. The first fish of each trip, we'd pour some beer down its mouth and throw him back with the directive to invite his larger relatives to the party we were having. I'm quite sure that had no effect on our fishing but it added to our story when talking about fishing in the kelp.

    We even took to driving up or down the coast, depending on our mood, looking for places where kelp beds grew, because where there was kelp, there was fish, or so we thought. You might think it grows along the entire coastline but it doesn't. The sea floor conditions and the amount of protection the area gets determined if the kelp would be able to take hold in the rocks and stay put during the winter storms.

    The kelp that grows along the pacific coast is the largest in the world and is referred to as sequoia kelp. A lot of the kelp is torn up during the winter and it winds up strewn on the beaches in great quantities. It's one of the "you get used to the smell of living at the beach" things.

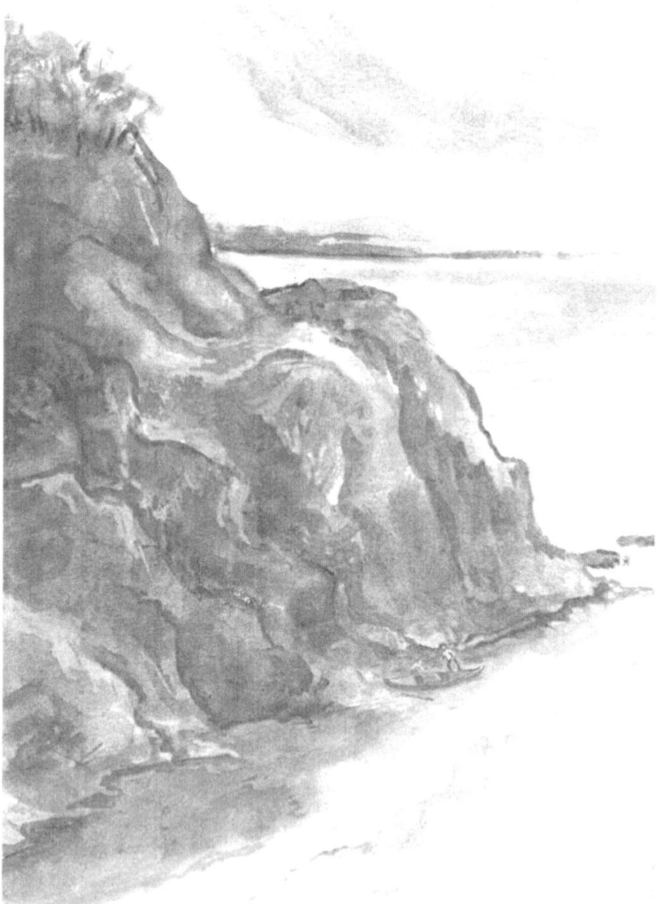

The Cliff Trail

Once we drove down the coast to Pismo Beach, because I had seen a huge kelp bed down there the week before. We had taken my boys down to go dirt bikin' and four wheeling. I ran the Widow Maker hill climb with the land cruiser. I had no idea if we could even get down to the beach anywhere close to where I saw the kelp bed. The coastline in that area tends to be a couple of hundred feet of vertical cliffs, straight into the water. Very spectacular scenery, but extremely dangerous to climb down. It's all loose sandstone and shell, making it treacherous. But we were hopeful that we could find a way as we drove the three hours down there.

You could see the kelp beds for miles along the shore, straight down two hundred feet or more. So, we doubled back up the highway looking for something like a way down; remember we had fishing gear, two boats, ice chests, and ourselves to get down there. We found what I'd call a goat trail, straight down the side of the cliff and there we went.

What Valerie and I did with the canoe was put everything in it and sort of let it slide down, her guiding the front and me acting as an anchor. We slipped vertically down the broken rocky trail to the beach. This should give you an inkling of what kind of maniacs the four of us were.

This kelp bed was miles long and we just knew after expending that much energy to get our stuff down that damn cliff, we were bound to catch a load of fish.

The surf wasn't bad and we were out and on our way in minutes, the sun was shining, there was a light breeze to cool us off from paddling and we were there. . . It was quite a bit farther than it looked from up on top of the hill out to the kelp.

But we finally got out there and started fishing. It didn't take us long until we realized that nobody was catching anything. We tried all our techniques to get the fish to bite but to no avail. The fish either weren't there or they weren't going to bite. So much for our theory that anywhere there's kelp there's fish! An hour went by, then another, still no fish. The girls were ready to go. But Ralph and I said "Let's stay just another hour then we'll go". After all, it had taken us over an hour just to get down the hill and we weren't ready to make the climb back up just yet!

Well, you guessed it; the wind came up out of nowhere, like it can do along the California Coast, when it blows offshore, coming from the hot inner valleys and being blown out over the cool sea. We call them "Santa Ana Winds". This one was only about forty miles an hour blowing us straight out to sea. We paddled with all our might for two straight hours against the wind before we got under the eve of the cliff. As the boats hit the sand we rolled out exhausted and lay there on the sand gasping for air. I couldn't help myself when I said "Are we having fun yet?" I was so winded; I wished I had saved my breath.

We decided it was time to drink up all the rest of the beer, so we didn't have to carry it back up the cliff.

Looking up from the bottom was completely disheartening. The road, three hundred feet away, up an 80 degree slope with only one small 60 degree stretch in the middle. Ten feet at a time was how we pulled and pushed each boat, there were grunts and groans aplenty. The boats loaded with our stuff moved slowly up the trail. I tell you, between the choking and coughing, slipping and sliding, it looked like a scene out of *Ben Hur* with only four slaves. The wind whipping the dust around that we were making made it even more miserable. We were generating our own dust storm and the Santa Anna wind was carrying it out to sea in a giant swirl rolling off the cliff and down to the surface of the water.

Finally, the top—and it was getting dark. We looked like four rag-a-muffins that had been fighting in the dirt all day. Dirty, tired, and disappointed, having gone to so much trouble and not having caught a thing. In fishing terms it's called "SKUNKED"!

It was a long quiet drive home that particular night. Val fell asleep almost as soon as the cruzer hit the road. Well, there was always tomorrow. . .

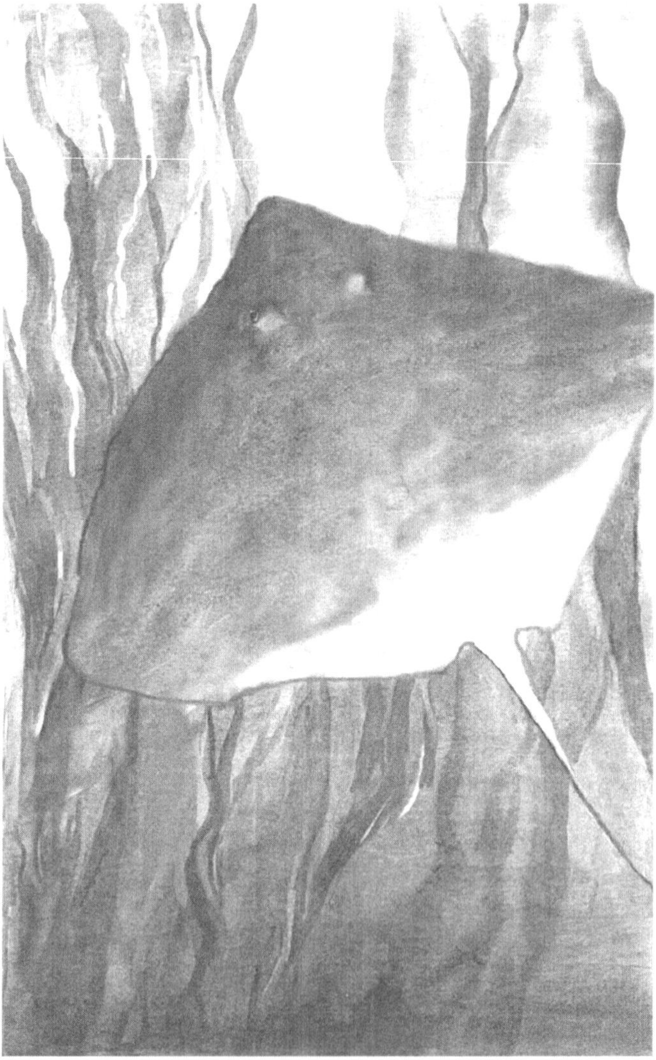

Making Scallops

One typically foggy morning Ralph and I were going out in our respective conveyances. As we left the world of visible landmarks and entered into the unending expanse of fog, we began to experience sensory deprivation. It's a frightening feeling that comes over you on the water when you can't tell which way is back. In one direction a half-mile or so is safety, in the other twenty thousand miles of water. I've experienced this even on a lake, where you know if you go in a straight line long enough, you'll get to the shore. In the ocean you have the direction of the swell as a reference, but that doesn't keep your senses from panicking when that last land disappears into the whiteness.

We had made our way out and up the coast to the far end of our little kelp forest and started fishing. It didn't take us long to catch five nice gopher cod. And shortly after, Ralph came over and tied up alongside, for a tequila break. We were at the edge of the kelp bed in an area where you can catch almost anything. The open water fish cruise the edges of the kelp bed looking for snacks.

As we sat there gabbing, Ralph's pole slammed down into the water. Something was peeling off the line. It was headed out into the open water of the bay. It took fifty yards of line before it ran out of gas. Finally, Ralph could start reeling it back in. We still didn't know what he had because it was running aground on the bottom and nothing Ralph could do seemed to do get it to come up at all. Well, we knew that eventually, Ralph would tire it out. So all he needed to do was keep it out of the kelp and wait. Twenty minutes this went on, and still we hadn't seen what was on the end of the line. Heck, Ralph was getting tired fighting this thing. Half an hour after it started, Ralph got the Skate up to the edge of the canoe. I'm saying, "Cut it loose,

Ralph, we don't want that thing in the boat." They're not good to eat, and they stink like you wouldn't believe. Ralph starts telling me about how he heard that you could cut plugs out of the wings that would taste like scallops. I said "That's ridiculous, Ralph".

"Oh no, I heard it from someone at school. Let's keep it and try cooking it".

"Then we're cooking it at your house, because I don't want that smell anywhere near my house." So we dragged the Skate onto the beach behind the kayak. After we got the boats on the dry sand, we got our scale out and weighed the thing; forty pounds and it was thirty-six inches across.

Valerie and I were invited over for dinner that night. When we pulled up at their apartment complex, we could smell that awful smell. Ralph had cut the plugs like the guy told him to, and when we got there he started to deep fry them. As soon as that stuff hit the oil, the entire apartment stunk up so bad we had to take the oil and skate out to the dumpster, where it rejoined the carcass and guts.

Well, that lesson learned: We had dinner that night at H Salt Fish and Chips.

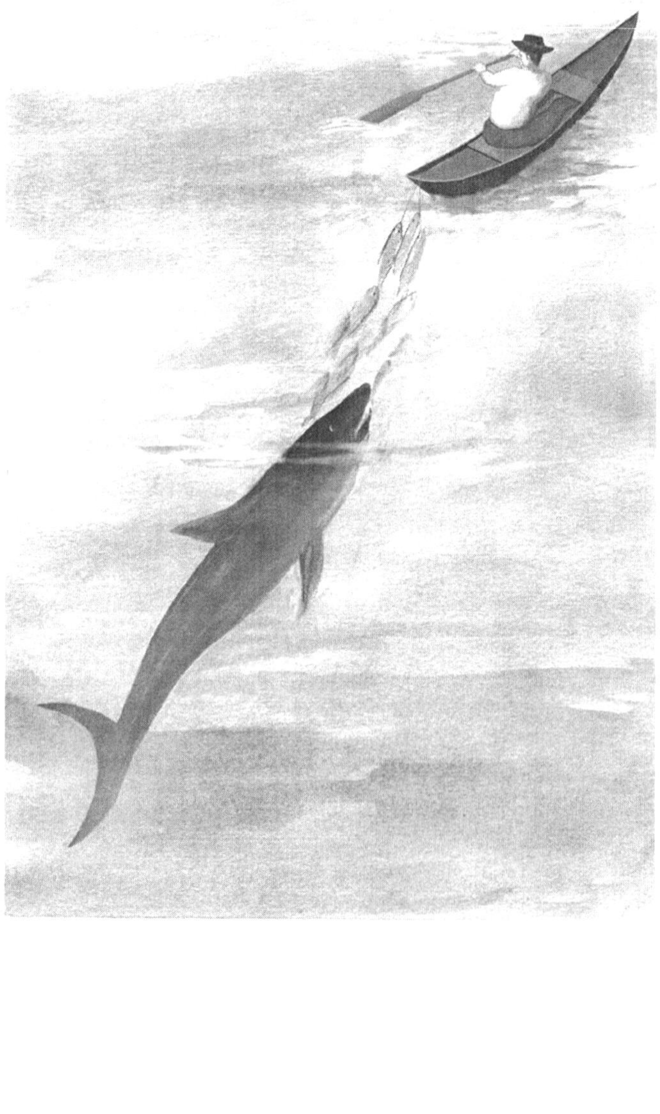

Whip Shot

The next time we went fishing that stands out as worth mentioning, it was a Saturday morning. Ralph and I met at the beach for a guy trip and we both brought our boats. We could have gone out together, and did several times, but we found that if we hunted separately, we covered more ground and therefore got more fish. By now, we had it down. It was like going to the store for fish with the added excitement of a canoe trip and being at the beach instead of the grocery store. There was the slight drawback of having to clean the fish, but I had learned how to do the Canadian-style filet, which has absolutely no bones in it at all. Throw in the great deal of practice that I'd been getting and some small amount of talent, filleting a small-to medium-size fish: two minutes flat. We always took them down to the cleaning stations on the concrete ship pier, which had running fresh water. If we wanted to fertilize the roses, I'd just throw the guts in a trash bag and take them home. We had thirty-five different roses in our rose garden.

We paddled out into the closest kelp bed and began fishing in our usual method of, "drop down, nobody home, move to the next kelp frown". It was slow and after an hour between us we had six fish of what we had come to call small cod, under three pounds, then nothing for an hour.

It's truly quiet out in the kelp beds. There is just little rustles of bubbles now and then coming off the kelp leaves, or the sound that the canoe makes pushing them out of its way as you move through the water. All the sounds of man were covered by the low rumble of the surf and the onshore breeze. It was easy to imagine going back in time a hundred or a thousand years. I often thought of the Indians that lived here, at one time there were more abundant life forms in Monterey

Bay than anywhere else on earth. It has to have been the Garden of Eden. No wonder I love coming out there. I would be transported from the cutting edge of technology to the trailing edge of time in moments. It's one of the places I found you didn't have to go far to get to "quiet and alone".

It was broken by Ralph's scream of "Oh my God!!!" I looked up to see Ralph being towed along the edge of the kelp bed, his reel peeling off line as he went. Whatever it was towed him fifty-yards in about a minute before he ran out of line and it snapped like a shot from a twenty-two rifle. Ralph just sat there stunned. After five minutes or so he started paddling back over to where I was. . . I had the beer and tequila. We both needed a break in the action, so we tied the boats together and drank up all the booze, discussed all possible theories on what it might have been and settled on a big SHARK.

It was that day we decided that we need to incorporate a gaffe in our fishing gear. If we ever got something that big up next to the boat what the hell would we do with it? So far, the biggest thing we had caught had to be the forty-pound skate which we had towed in behind Ralph's kayak; which leads into our next encounter for *THE BIG FISH HUNTERS*.

You know, you never know what you might catch in the ocean. So if you're one of us who uses eighty-pound test line and stainless steel leaders . . . Be prepared!

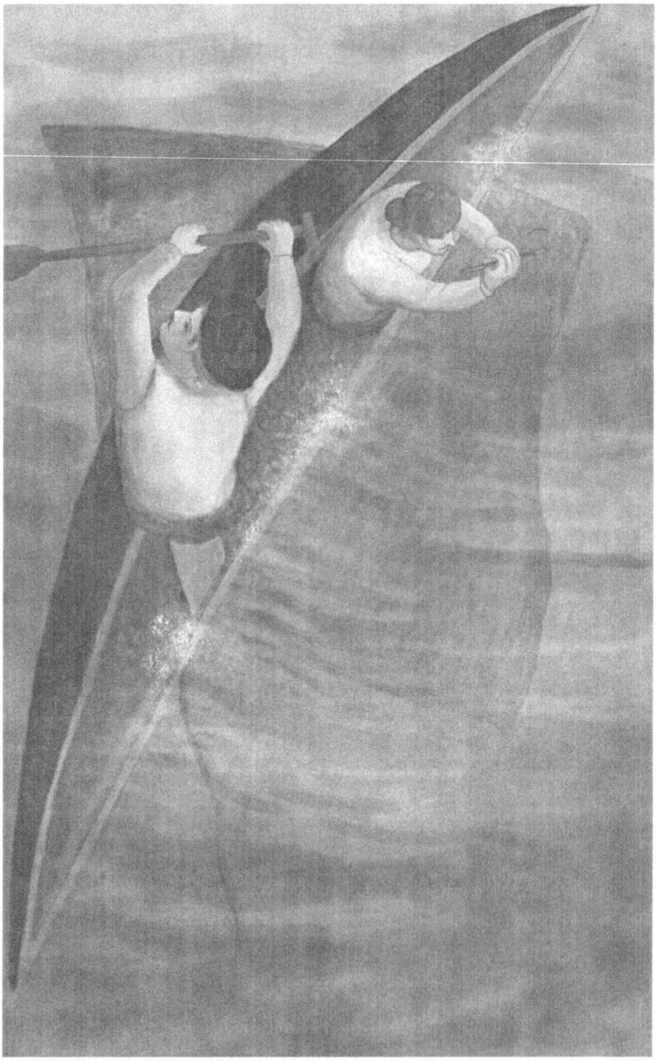

Who's Got Who

It didn't take the mighty *BIG FISH HUNTERS* long to encounter their next memorable quarry.

In this encounter, Ralph and I were in the canoe, the fishing had been fair. We had ten nice gopher cod, which were the main inhabitants of the kelp beds. Things came to a stop and we moved several times with no more luck. We went back to the edge of the kelp bed, on our way in, and stopped again. Five minutes later my boat pole slammed into the side of the canoe. It spun us around and started pulling us; we headed straight into deeper water. I was content to let it wear itself out in the open water, which it did. Finally, I started making headway on reeling it in. Mind you, we still hadn't seen what this thing was . . . Ralph in true *BIG FISH HUNTER* style got the gaffe and put the loop around his wrist in preparation for the kill. This thing ran around under the canoe for another ten minutes. I told Ralph "I think it's getting tired. Man, I know I am."

Ralph was looking over the side of the canoe waiting to get his first look at what I'd been fighting. Here comes something up next to the side of the canoe and he slams the gaffe into it.

All hell breaks loose, in the canoe and underneath it. Ralph's yelling "I got—I got—" However, he can't see the other side of the canoe, and whatever he has is on both sides of our boat. It's a ray or a skate that had to be six feet across and probably four hundred pounds. I said very quietly "Ralph, I think it has you." I had to lean completely out of my side of the canoe to keep Ralph from being pulled out of the boat and into the water. Ralph looked like a rodeo bull rider hanging on for dear life. Ralph's arm was pulled straight out one second, and back under the canoe the next. This thing pulled us back and forth for five minutes. Ralph was now screaming "Oh my God Oh my God!" over and over. He couldn't get his hand out of the loop and it looked like the ray had caught its second wind. It was about to leave the area with Ralph still attached to the gaffe. Just as the canoe started to turn over, Ralph, already pulled halfway into the water, manages to get the loop off his wrist. His face was in the water on his side. When he got free, I went face first into the water on my side. I wasn't quick enough to re-balance us in time. We were half sunk. The ray left with the gaff. We managed to save the canoe from going all the way over but it was half-full of water and we were both soaked to the bone. All Ralph could say was "JESUS, that thing almost broke my arm!" We bailed most of the water out, had a beer and headed for the beach. The remaining gaff had the wrist loop removed when we went out the next time. The thinking was, if you couldn't get it in the boat with one hand you probably didn't want it in the boat.

We began to notice that the size and type of fish changed as the season rolled by. The main change was, the Ling cod came in to spoon, we hadn't caught any of them all summer. At first they were not much bigger than the fish we had gotten used to catching; these ranged from two to five pounds. Then the first seven-pound Ling brought on a celebration and fish fry. For the next two months we caught ten-to fifteen-pound Lings sprinkled in with the Gopher Cod which were also bigger in the winter.

    The fish were not the only things bigger in the winter. The surf was getting huge. Over the course of the summer we had gotten good at going out and in through surf. But the winter swells put our skills and our nerves to the test, every time we went. We had started off on two-foot waves, now we were up to six-and eight-footers. And I must admit it was awesome to be able to surf the canoe in on those kinds of waves. I'm pretty sure we started the kayak-in-the-surf craze because before us I'd never seen anyone do it, and I spent a lot of time at the beach.

88   *The Ultimate Fish Story*

Mean Green

This time I was out by myself. When you are the only one in the canoe you have to sit in the middle which makes the front lighter. The surf was huge, the wave front twelve feet high. The only reason I could get through surf that big was that the duration between the waves was quite long. There are a lot of variables that make up surf conditions; two variables are the size of the swells and the duration between them. If the swells had been close together I wouldn't have had time to get out past the breaking point. As it was, the canoe punched through the top of the breaking wave. I managed to get my paddle into the green water and pull as the rest of the wave broke over me. I'm sure it looked like the atomic submarine blasting straight up out of the water when the canoe came through the top of the wave. The rest of the wave broke over me. I had to paddle like crazy to get off the lip of the wave. It sucked me backwards twenty feet or so as it rolled to the beach, making the distance between me and the top of the next wave I needed to get over almost farther than I could cover. Paddling as fast as I could, I was near the limit of my endurance when I topped the next wave. But I managed to get out through it and only slightly wet.

 I sat just outside the surf line catching my breath, but I was out, the air cool and crisp, the rumble of the surf in the background, and there were fish to be caught. I started at the usual place and worked my way around the kelp beds, picking up three moderate size Gophers.

 The swell was making fishing down through the kelp difficult. It tended to push the kelp back and forth. The trick to fishing in the kelp is to be able to pull the fish straight up without letting it get tangled in the kelp. The shallow water and the swells were making it difficult not to be tangled.

    I lost several lost baits in the swirling kelp so I picked up and moved out into deeper water. We had found that in the bigger swell and in the wind too, you could tie the canoe to the kelp to keep you from moving. After all, you had to fish straight down so moving was bad!

    I got out to the edge of the outside kelp bed and tied the canoe up, opened a beer and had a shot of tequila, and knew the world was right. I no more got my line down to the bottom when I caught my first big Ling. Well, to me it was the biggest thing I'd caught so far. It turned out to be seventeen pounds of mean green with a set of teeth you can't believe in a fish that's not a shark. We had had to add heavy gloves and a large pair of channel-lock pliers to the arsenal of things we used to defend ourselves against the fish we were catching.

    I got this one on the stringer and tied it back to the canoe. Had a shot of tequila for my good fortune and got back to the tasks at hand. Three or four minutes went quietly by, so I was doing some cleaning up after catching the last fish. I had moved up to the middle of the canoe to wipe it down. I'd learned not to leave my fishing pole loose in the canoe as they had a tendency to just jump over the side and take off if not fastened down, so it was stuck under the rear seat. It was sticking out over the side of the canoe about three feet.

Something hit it so hard that the pole bounced a foot in the air before slamming down against the canoe rail and bending into the water. Not only that, it was sinking the canoe when I got in the back to try to get the pole. I could see the canoe going down a couple of inches every time the fish pulled. I couldn't seem to get the pole out from under the seat and back into the middle of the boat where I had a better chance of not sinking. Finally with water pouring in the canoe, I got the reel turned over and yanked it out from under the seat. The end of this little boat pole still hadn't come out of the water. I got back into the middle of the canoe which gave me the whole canoe to pull against. I was leaning over the opposite side like an outrigger against this fish. The canoe at this point had about two inched of water in it.

I had no idea how big this thing was, but it was big. I began it think I was actually going to land this fish if it didn't get tangled up. It pulled me twenty feet through the kelp before it ran out of gas. It just stopped pulling, and sat there on the bottom. It was all I could do to get this thing to move toward the surface.

I looked like I was fighting a Marlin; pull up reel, pull up reel, it was coming though. I was watching the kelp to see what I was bringing up next to my canoe. Eight feet away the kelp started to part like a submarine was going through. Its head was as large as a basket ball and I couldn't tell how long it might be. I took a couple of deep breaths and decided to let it stay under the water for a minute while I figured out what to do.

Well, I came out there to claim the *BIG FISH HUNTER* title and there it was, four feet away. This thing was a monster; I still didn't know how long it was, having only seen the business end of it. I got the gaff and put the loop around my wrist,(I know, my bad). I had let the monster set two feet under the canoe while I got ready. It was now or never—it might get rested up again and I didn't want that. I took a deep breath, got the gaff down in front of my victim. I knew I was inches away from the title. This gaff had to be perfect; this monster was mine. . . Just like that the gaff was through its lower jaw and I was looking down at it hanging by the gaff against the side of the canoe. I had to get both hands on the gaff to try to get that fish into the canoe. I couldn't lift it into the canoe completely. I struggled to pull the monster over the side of the canoe. The canoe rolled toward the fish and the rail went slightly under the water. The fish slipped toward me—and the only way it could have happened, the fish was in the canoe. A little water came in with the fish but there it was, filling up the entire front of the canoe. Jesus, what a set of teeth, these teeth were over an inch and a half long across the front of her mouth. It was hands down the largest fish any of us landed, forty-four pounds of Mean Green. We called her that because the female's meat was really green; it turned white, though, when you cooked it. The male's meat looked like any other fishes, white. I got the other three fish in the canoe and tied them all together on the middle thwart. The front of the canoe was full of Ling Cod with just those four fish.

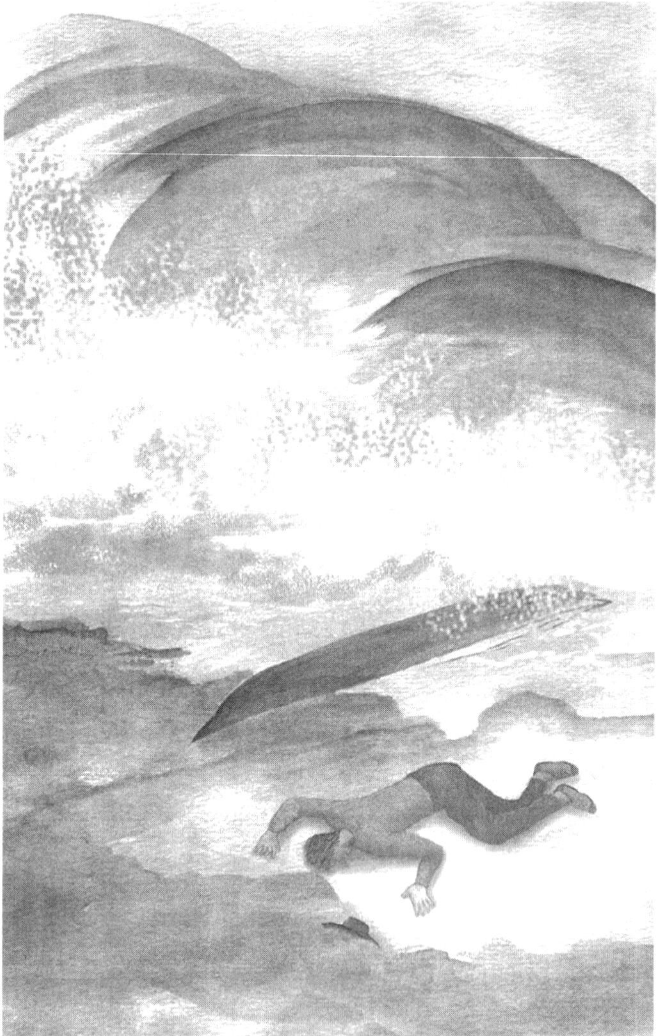

The Price of Fame

Unbeknownst to me, four hours had gone by; I hadn't noticed the swell steadily getting bigger. Now that I was headed back into shallower water I got a sinking feeling that this could be dangerous to my health. The sound of the surf was now deafening and I could feel the canoe shake from the waves pounding the beach. The air had gotten thick with salt spray and a sinister haze hung over the beach. I was sitting just outside where the waves were forming, that spot you see the surfer sitting waiting for a wave. I really knew that I didn't belong out here in these giant waves. I paddled out a little farther, got out the tequila bottle and finished it. No sense in losing it if the ice chest came open in a crash, which by now I was fairly sure was going to happen. Finally I couldn't wait anymore. I eased up to the surf line looking over my shoulder, not for the biggest swell but a place where I didn't see one. They were all really big.

Finally, I decided I'd go behind the next one. Maybe I could slip all the way in to the beach. The wave passed under the canoe. I let it get a few feet in front of me when I, too, took off. I wanted to stay just behind this wave and in front of the next one.

The wave outran me. The next one started to pick up the canoe and push it. I was riding the wave for a couple of seconds before the canoe started to turn sideways. There was nothing I could do; I went completely sideways. I was dragging my paddle in the face of the wave to keep the canoe from rolling but that didn't last long. When the wave face got to me, it exploded and started rolling the canoe over and over. Out in front of this twelve foot wall of moving water, tumbling me like a little stick in the foam the wave makes. I had had everything tied into the canoe except the paddle and me which had been thrown into the icy water on the first roll.

Now, here you have twelve-foot waves and an idiot with a canoe full of fish trying to get to shore. This is more difficult and dangerous than you might expect, for there are unseen forces of nature at work in the surf. For me the worst one was that the water was being pushed down the beach; an undertow pulling everything with it, canoe, fish, and me.

At one point I had to let the canoe go its own way. I was drowning in the foam of the wave. I needed to get into water I could swim in or at least stand up in at part of the time. I needed some air that wasn't half water. So I swam after the canoe. I really thought I might drown that afternoon but I hadn't written the story yet.

The spectacle of being dragged half a mile through the gigantic surf seems like it took forever to end. Half frozen, completely exhausted, and out of adrenaline, I finally caught up with the canoe and dragged it up on the beach. I couldn't move any more. I sat there for half an hour getting my breath and strength back. I was blue from the cold but the monster fish was still tied to the canoe. My title as *BIG FISH HUNTER* was guaranteed. The riptide and the huge surf had made a little slough behind the sand bar where the big surf was breaking. I rolled the canoe up on its side to get the water and sand out. I saw the paddle laying thirty-yards farther down the beach, so I staggered off to retrieve it.

It was a slow walk pulling the canoe back up toward the pier, but the evidence, the proof to the title, was lying in the bottom of that canoe. "*BIG FISH HUNTER*"—that's me. The little slew was only half way back to the pier so in three trips across the sand I got everything back to the land cruiser.

Carrying those fish on my canoe paddle you'd have thought I was Caesar coming into Rome. There were a lot of people there to witness the soaking wet fisherman with the giant fish. And yes, most of them saw the crash in the surf.

This was the last trip for the winter, as most days the surf was even bigger. It was not unusual to have ten-to fifteen-foot waves in the winter; if they got down to five or six feet it was small. During a storm I had seen, waves over thirty-five feet shaking the ground for two or three miles inland.

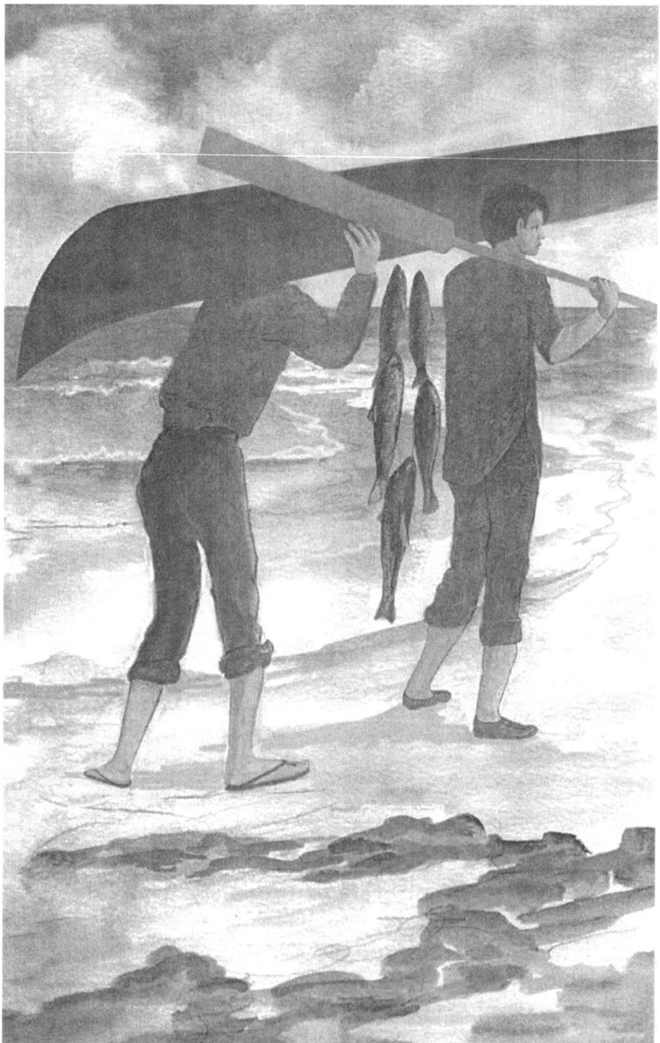

The Kids

The local teenage kids all hung out at my house. Why? Because I let them drink beer there, so I could keep an eye on them. Their parents were grateful too, at least they knew where their kids were and that they were not likely to get into too much trouble.

They all wanted to get a chance to go out in the canoe so they too could be *BIG FISH HUNTERS*. That summer while school was out, I started taking one of them with me when I went. There were four of them hanging around with my son that summer. Gene, my oldest boy, wanted nothing to do with fishing or eating fish. He never got to go. As for the rest of 'm, they all went several times, except for big

Mike. Mike had all the enthusiasm you might ever need, but absolutely no sense of balance, which is, after all, the main ingredient required in canoeing.

Mike's one trip was one of the wettest ones I ever made. We rolled the canoe three or four times trying to get out and the surf wasn't all that big. My dad used to have a phrase "like a bull in a china shop". I couldn't keep the canoe balanced against Mike's weight. He was two-twenty against my one-sixty, it just didn't add up. There we were, completely soaked by the time we managed to get the canoe past the waves and out to the kelp beds. We were laughing our heads off, though, while we wrung the water out of our socks. I was so grateful to tie the canoe up to the kelp, break out a beer, and follow it by a couple of shots of tequila. It seemed to make the wet clothes not as uncomfortable. Actually, the whole thing was hilarious.

We were setting there, taking off our shirts and wringing them over the side of the canoe, all the time laughing like a couple of crazies. I'll give Mike that; he was always easy to make laugh.

Finally, we got down to fishing. And, as fishing trips go, it turned out to be a great trip. We caught eight nice Gophers and a keepable Ling apiece.

I was dreading going back in. I just knew we were going to get wet again. Like I said, in a canoe balance is first. Second is weight distribution fore and aft. Having more weight in the front caused the canoe to easily ride the wave straight into the beach, although Mike almost dumped us when the wave picked up the canoe and started moving it. I was yelling at him "Mike, Mike, just be still. Let me drive this thing from back here." The wave deposited us on the sand. We stepped out, picked up the canoe and carried it twenty feet above the water's edge and parked it.

Mike got to carry the fish and answer all the questions. We were always asked about where, how, and when the fish had been caught, every time we came in with a stringer of fish. They all said they had never seen so many fish caught at this beach. Nobody caught as many fish as we did; nobody.

We cleaned the fish at the Concrete Ship and used the fish guts to fertilize my roses. I had thirty-one different varieties of roses surrounding my little house, the picture book cottage by the sea. My little redwood house with the roses in the front yard made all the local home magazines.

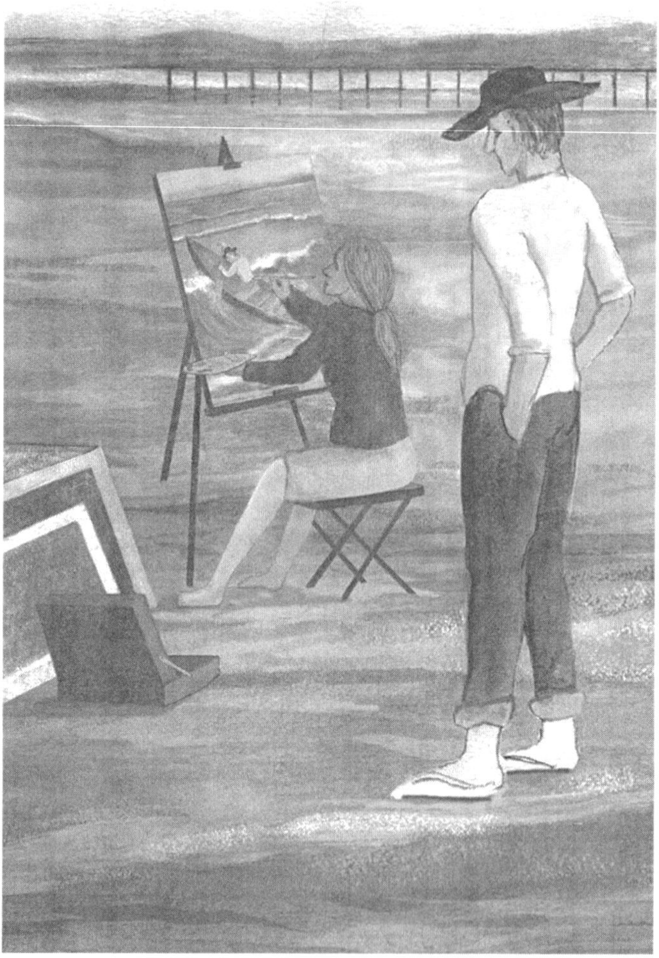

The Painting

One trip out, I had caught four or five Gopher Cod and was loading my stuff in the land cruiser. I noticed this lady painting seascapes of the beach. I had seen her down there quite a few times over the course of the summer. I really had not paid much attention to what she was painting. Although, once I walked close enough to see a seascape of the Capitola Pier along with part of the coastline and some clouds. You know, typical beach landscape paintings. Today, she was close to where I parked; I saw she had painted *me*, sitting out in the canoe, fishing in the kelp. She had included my old brown Stetson cowboy hat pulled down in front, me slumped over with the little white boat pole sticking out over the side of the canoe, sitting in the kelp bed. There were some small waves in the foreground and a few puffy clouds overhead to complete the picture.

She had several different size paintings with me as the subject. I could see she had several larger ones she had done neatly arranged in a holder standing up in her van.

I asked her, "How much for the one you're finishing up?" It was two-by three feet or so; she said, "two hundred dollars". I told her didn't have any money on me. So I proposed trading her the fish I had caught, for the littlest painting. She wanted thirty dollars for it and I knew the fish weren't worth that, but she agreed to the trade. It was eight by ten inches and I took it home and hung it up on the wall with another boat painting.

Two weeks later Val and I happened into the Capitola Pier bar and there I was, immortalized in paint behind the bar. The biggest painting she had done, three by five feet of me. I really had become a famous fisherman.

112   *The Ultimate Fish Story*

Raining Trout

    One of the places Val and I stopped to fish on our honeymoon trip through Canada was Eagle Fly Lake. When we got there it seemed pretty nondescript, as Canadian lakes go. We got there late in the day, just before the sun sinks below the horizon. We unloaded the canoe and slipped it into the water. Then we went about making camp and pitching our tent. As the last rays of sun reflected off the glacier to the west, the sky lit up with streams of rainbow color that streaked across the sky. The little non-descript lake was transformed into a wonderland of Kodachrome color and reflections.

Next morning, we were up early as usual, and when we opened the tent front we were met with a dense wet fog. We clamored out and began the morning task of making breakfast. The smell of campfires burning cedar added to cold crisp air. Breakfast was trout filets and eggs smothered in onions, yum. Afterward, we took our plates and skillet down to the edge of the lake to clean up. The fog lay so dense on the surface that we could hardly see past the end of our canoe. That's thick.

Chores done, it was time to select our weapon of the day. We both had several different-style fishing poles to choose from, depending on what the occasion called for or how we felt on that day. Our small fly rods had been getting the most use on this trip. Decisions made, we headed out on the lake. We kept hearing these little splashes, just out of sight, hidden in the fog. You know how it sounds like when it first starts to rain, the drops are huge right before the downpour. It seemed to come from all directions at once. We couldn't figure out what might be making the sounds. We hadn't been hit by any rain drops.

We headed over to some reeds and tried fishing along the bank, no luck. We moved out deeper into the lake to try trolling the lines out behind the canoe.

We were just paddling along in the fog when this trout jumped out of the lake and landed in the floor of canoe. It about scared us both half to death. Things aren't supposed to land in your canoe out on the lake; it's unsettling. Both of us jumped at the same time. That fear of turning over is always in the back of your mind. At first glance I couldn't see what it was. I just heard it flopping in the bottom of the canoe. When I got to it, I picked it up and put it back in the lake. It wasn't very big at all.

We still hadn't caught any fish after two hours. We were getting bored; the fog had started to lift, literally. You could see it lifting slowly off the surface of the water. As it lifted, we could see these three-inch bubbles of gray setting on the surface of the lake. The fog had been captured in the bubbles. There was a foot, then slowly rising up to four feet of visibility, where it stopped.

Now we could see what was making the splashes. Across the entire lake, fish were jumping out of the water. It looked like it was raining fish. You know how the water rises up after the drop hits and sometimes makes a bubble on the surface. The bubbles across the entire lake were slowly changed from gray, filled with fog, to clear, as the fog rose. When the fog-filled bubble burst a little cloud streamed upward. We'd never seen anything like it and probably won't ever again.

Well, we couldn't catch anything, so we went back to camp. There was a group of locals camped next to us, we could tell by their accents. So we went over to inquire about what was going on, on the lake. They told us the lake had gotten a parasite. It was attacking the trout population. The poor trout were jumping out of the water to try to get away from the stinging, biting critters. They also told us the Canadian Fish and Game was due to come up here and kill the lake. That's the only way to get rid of the parasite. They had to kill everything in the lake including the plants that grew there.

The lake would be barren for three years after the poisoning.

This parasite was not indigenous to Canada; someone had dumped something into the lake. More and more this happens to our wilderness areas and lakes. Someone not thinking about the consequences of what they're doing contaminates or introduces something into our environment that takes over and ruins the balance of nature.

There's a plant from Asia that's choking a third of the Canadian waterways. The entire area must be poisoned, killing everything in the water for years afterwards to rid the infestation.

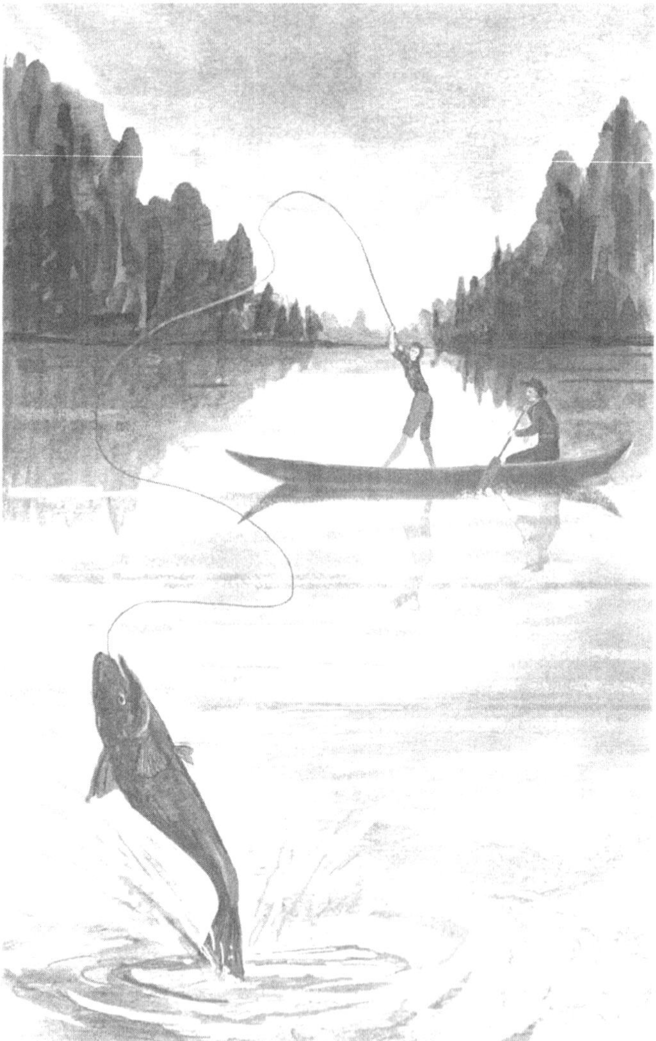

Valerie's Balancing Act

Our next stop was Crystal Lake, a huge lake with an island off to one end. It was probably fifteen miles long with two of those being the island. We almost always left one spot in the mid-morning arriving at the next in the late afternoon or early evening. We wanted enough light left in the day to get our tent pitched and camp stuff set up.

There were several groups of Canadians camping there too. So when we were done with our chores, we went over to check out the fishing report on the lake. We had found each lake had some unique aspects to it, and if you wanted to catch fish, you needed to know their whereabouts and their preferences. One of the groups had a guide that was familiar with this lake. He was most helpful with filling us in on what to use and where to use it. He told us the fish would be thick over an artesian well that fed the far end of the lake. It was a hundred yards or so off the southern end of the island. Well, that made it about twelve miles to paddle just to get down there.

The next morning we were up early and off to the other end of the lake. We paddled and paddled. We rested and paddled. I think our best speed might have been four miles an hour. By the time we got there, which was around mid-morning, we were both tired of paddling. The guide was right. Everyone on the lake was fishing in a little group off the end of the island.

Valarie was still learning how to fly fish. She was having trouble getting the line to layout, sitting down in the canoe. So she said "Harry, I need to stand up to do this. Sitting down just isn't working!"

"I don't Know, Val," I said. "Standing up in a canoe. . ."

"If I can do back-flips on a six-inch-wide balance beam, I bet I can stand up in this canoe".

So I said, "Hang on for second, let me put my pole up and get the paddle out to help stabilize the canoe." This done, she turned and started to stand. A little wobble or two and she slowly stood up. This was incredible. She twisted around a little with her hands out for balance but I could see she was getting the hang of it. After several minutes of practice just standing, she raised her fly rod and proceeded to lay out sixty feet of fly line without any apparent difficulty.

There were a dozen other boats that witnessed this. They all stopped fishing to get their cameras out. Everybody with a camera wanted to take pictures of this crazy California girl standing up fly-fishing in a canoe. On her third cast she had a fish on. She promptly sat down and we landed her fish. This was great; I was having more fun watching her and watching the others watch her than fishing. I was more than happy to just balance the canoe for her.

The fish was landed and on the stringer. She was up again, laying out perfectly straight lines. Four or five minutes went by without any action. Then she dubbed flipped to the same spot, the fly barely touching the water the first time. As the fly was coming down the second time a huge trout jumped out of the water to meet the fly three feet in the air. It broke the line when it took off and pulled Val off balance. She over-corrected from the unexpected jerk on her rod and almost swamped the canoe, but she hung on. I managed to prevent the canoe from going over far enough to throw her out, but we were half swamped.

Three of the other boats came over to see if we were O.K. or needed any help. It was getting late, so after we bailed out most of the water we asked one of the guides for a tow back up the lake. He was more than happy to oblige, although he had never towed anything behind his canoe. He had an eighteen-foot square-ender canoe with a little eight-horse Evinrude to push it. He started us out slow, afraid to go every fast. It was difficult to keep us straight with Val in the front so I had him stop and

Val got in the back with me. This raised the nose, and I told our new friend "wide open" all the way home.

It still took half an hour to get back. The drone of the little Evinrude prompted us to make up the Evinrude song. . . It had one note. "And the Evinrude went huuuummmmm" . . . We were so grateful to be towed back down the lake. We had exhausted ourselves this day and added a great deal to our story, including some great new friends.

That night all the campers came over to chat. Mainly to see the only person they'd ever witnessed fly fishing standing up in a canoe. Val made the cover of one of the Canadian fishing magazines the next month. The caption said "Check out this girl's balance". It was a picture of her standing up in the canoe, fish three feet out of the water, rod bent over against the fish. Incredible!

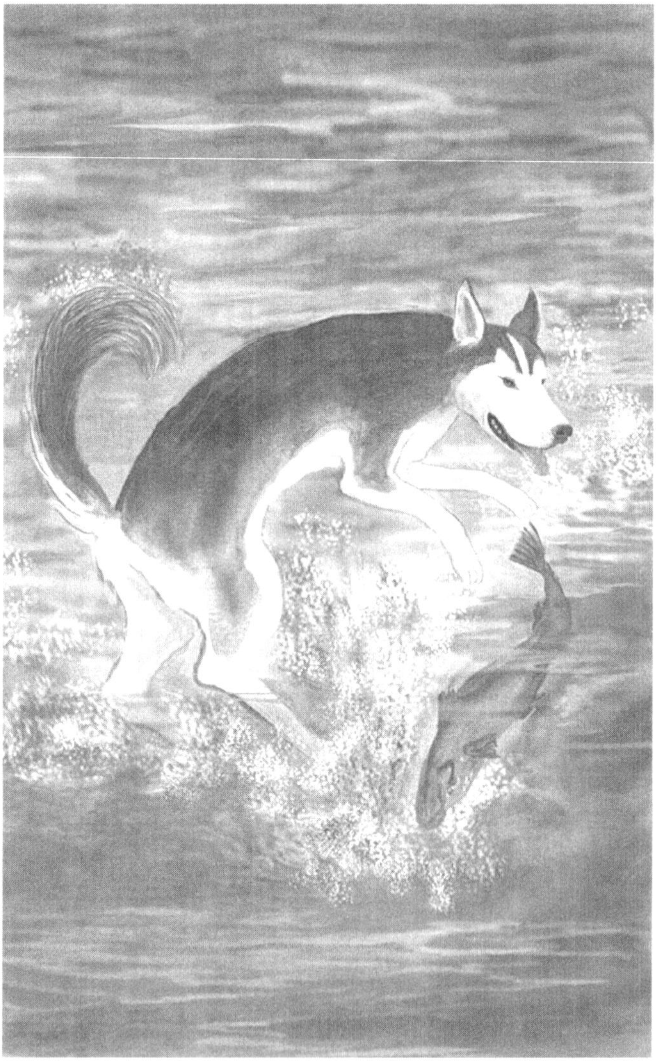

Kowa's Canoe Training

Getting ready for our month-long adventure on the Frazier river, we started taking Kowa canoe camping. Kowa was our ninety-pound Samoyed Husky.

From a tiny puppy he went with me everywhere. His spot in the land cruiser started off in the console. When he outgrew that he naturally moved to passenger seat. At work he sat next to my desk while I was working, and when I took a break so did he. Kowa was extremely smart, and learned not only voice commands but hand signals like the dogs in Hollywood movies have to do. He knew all the regular dog tricks just like Lassie and a few more that were truly remarkable. His best one, though, was being shot: I'd make a gun with my hand, make sure he saw it and point it at him. When I pulled up my hand like a gun being shot He'd throw his legs out from under him and hit the ground with his eyes closed and head down. The only thing moving would be his tail, it would be slowly wagging. I'd say "dead dog's tails don't wag" and it would flop down and stay motionless. Dog and tail would lie there until the O.K. command was given; he was definitely a ham.

He'd been camping with us, but not on a canoe camping trip. He'd have to get used to riding in the canoe all day; of course we'd stop often to let him and ourselves out to stretch, and take care of other business. We picked a big lake in southern Oregon that had an island at one end. We wanted to make it a day's paddle to our campsite, and this place fit the bill. A park and camp grounds were at the northern end of the lake, a lodge with a boat dock about ten miles down from there, and another five miles on down to the island. The weatherman had predicted beautiful weather for the next three days. We'd spend one day getting there, one camping, and one getting back and loading up for home. That was the plan.

Kowa was all over the canoe at the start, but soon settled down in the middle and snoozed on and off as Val and I slowly made our way down the lake. We hung in next to the shore so we could stop occasionally for a break. On a river trip you don't do as much paddling as on a lake. But we figured if we could paddle all day, we'd be in good shape for our trip.

We got to the island at dusk and hurriedly set about making our campsite. Kowa bounded out of the canoe and had to go mark off his area. Then he took off running. He was back in eight or nine minutes. This was the first time he'd run on a beach that came back to where you started. He was surprised when he burst out of the trees to find himself back at camp. So he ran around the other way to see if it happened again. It did.   He must have decided it was too much to ponder and went to play in the water while Valarie while I made dinner. We had brought lots of freeze-dried foods to sample. We wanted to know which ones we'd like, as some were actually quite good, which leaves the ones that weren't.

The next morning we were up early as usual. We had brought waders with us, another first for Kowa. Valarie and I waded out into the water and started fishing, Kowa came right behind us. I guess he thought he needed to be out there with us. I finally got him to go back up to the tent and lay down. He was laying up there watching us fish.

When Val caught a fish, here came Kowa. Val was getting the fish in close for me to net, when Kowa decided he's a retriever. He jumped in trying to bite the fish. He didn't stand a chance in actually catching it, but he made a whole bunch of tries. Biting the water and jumping backward like he had it. It was truly comical, the fishing dog. The great thing about Kowa was, all I had to do was tell him to stay in the camp that afternoon and he didn't bug us anymore.

We fished through the afternoon with some success; we both caught our dinner fish. It was always better to mix real food in with the freeze-dried stuff anyway.

I was watching the clouds build over the mountains as the evening approached. It was supposed to be clear for our trip. We were awakened by the sound of wind whipping the tent around before sunrise, and it was blowing out of the north. Of course, that was the direction we had to go back to our transportation; all that way back up the lake against this wind. Well, maybe it would die down for us? It didn't.

We packed our camp and loaded the canoe to leave, the wind still blowing. It was only fifteen-to twenty-miles per hour as we pushed off and headed out into the lake. It soon became apparent getting back had become a monumental undertaking. After three hours of paddling as hard and constant as we could, we'd made maybe five miles, and the wind and waves were getting worse. Kowa had been good up to this point but I think he knew Valarie and I were getting nervous about the conditions. We were literally being pushed backward now by the thirty-mile-an-hour wind and four-foot waves.

As the first wave broke over the bow cover and spilled into Val's lap, Kowa decided it was time to bail out as his riding area had just gotten wet. He was sliding around as the canoe rolled in the waves, trying to get poised to jump over board. He undoubtedly would have capsized us on his way out. I had to stop paddling, and grab Kowa before he managed to jump, push his head down between my feet and reassure him he needed to " Stay, puppy" which he did.

We were now sideways and taking water with every wave. I decided to angle in toward the shore keeping as much of the bow into the waves as possible. By now we were all wet from the wind and waves. Now, it started to rain on top of that.

We managed to get to the lodge pier and pulled underneath it, out of the rain. After tying the canoe up next to a ladder, I lifted Kowa up on the pier. He was eye level with me when he paid me back by shaking all that water right in my face. He was happy to be out of that canoe and on something that wasn't moving. Val and I were equally glad that we had made it off the lake without losing anything.

The owners of the lodge said they had been watching us out there with utter amazement and were just about to come out and rescue us when we headed in.

They were so kind. They let us wrap up in bath towels while they threw our clothes in the dryer.

We spent the night there. The little storm blew through during the late afternoon but Val and I were not inclined to venture out that late. Next morning was beautiful, sun shining, birds chirping, and we had made some new friends. It was an easy trip back to the land cruiser and a wonderful ride back home. We had added yet another adventure to our collection.

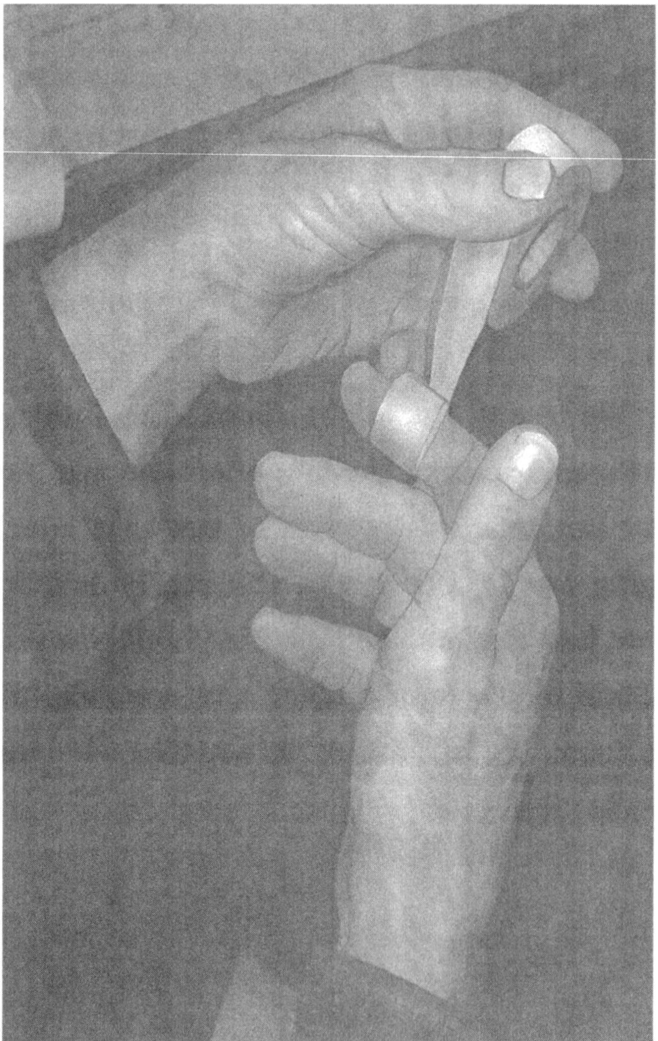

Dad's Day

My dad passed away in 1988. He was an avid outdoorsman; when he went fishing or hunting, more often than not, he took his two oldest sons with him if not all three of us. I was the oldest, followed by Jack, a year younger, and Steve, five years behind Jack.

I went on a lot of hunting and fishing trips with my dad, as I was an extra limit of whatever was on the menu. Wherever we went we always camped out. All my life I wanted to do something extraordinary for my parents. My Dad's gift had to be the ultimate fishing trip. Valarie and I had found the place: Canada.

When Valerie and I had gone on our honeymoon to Canada the year before, someone had told us how to find this little artesian spring feed lake. It was high up in a mountain saddle, almost impossible to get to, unless you had a four-wheel-drive vehicle; we did.

The really cool thing was that the little lake had a crescent shape bending around a four-hundred-foot vertical peak on one side and two sheer cliffs on the other. There was a narrow slit between the two cliffs for the four-wheel drive tail to get through. The surrounding topology kept the float planes from getting in and spoiling it.

We had pulled our land cruiser behind dad's van up from California. We stopped at the bottom of the mountain cutoff to unhook it, and reconnect the drive shift. That done, we started up the four-wheel-drive trail. Val and I went first. I'd stop after a particularly nasty section and wait for dad and mom in the van.

We were impressed: with a running start and enough horsepower the van made most of the trip up the rutted twisting trail by itself. Near the top, however, it slipped sideways and came to rest against a tree. So we hooked up the jump strap between the two and in four-wheel low eased the van the rest of the way up the trail.

A little downhill jog found us at a beautiful campsite, right next to the lake. It seemed to be cut out of the forest, a grassy flat spot. It was truly a photograph waiting to be taken. The mountain's reflection in the mirror still lake. You couldn't tell where one ended and the reflection started.

We set up our tents, unloaded the gear and got the canoes into the water. Val and I were dying to catch something in this beautiful setting. Mom and Dad were just glad to be out of the van and able to walk around a little.

Valarie and I were used to fly fishing for rainbow trout in the lakes at home. There, we caught fish in the ten-to twenty ounce range. Not knowing any better, I got out my fly rod, set up a tippet with one-pound test and selected a sinking brown fly. A few quick flips and the line laid out straight as an arrow and began sinking. Two seconds later something hit it and broke the tippet.

Val scolded me for not having any finesse with the rod. A moment later she had the same thing happen.

Well, time to adjust our strategy, two-pound tippets was the heaviest we had; that broke. Between the tippet and the fly line we used five-pound test, so I tied the fly directly on. Sure enough, the next fish stayed on almost back to the canoe.

Enough is enough; we went back to camp and raided my dad's supplies. He had a spool of fifteen-pound test, no tippet this time. I tied the fly with fifteen-pound test straight to the fly line! I was going to see what it was we were trying to catch. It worked. The fish was twenty-six inches long and weighed eight pounds, not bad for the first fish of the trip. I brought the fish up to the side of the canoe, reached down and got my dip net. I looked at the fish, looked at the net. The fish was way too big for my dip net. The net was fine for California trout or trout in general, but these fish were actually landlocked salmon which can reach two hundred pounds. Instead, I got a rag, wrapped it around my hand and grabbed the fish by the mouth. I wasn't losing this one. It turned out to be one of the smaller ones by the end of our stay.

Well, we ate that fish for dinner that night, and had scrambled eggs and trout the next morning for breakfast. After breakfast we headed out: Mom and Dad went one way, Val and I the other. It was going to be a glorious fishing adventure this day. Val and I started off fly-fishing in the usual manner that one fishes with a fly rod, laying out your line, and twitching the fly on the end, waiting a moment and twitching it again as the fly sinks. We were working along a section of reeds around the edge of the lake. Val would stand in the canoe and fish while I kept us steady, but we didn't have any luck using this method.

We decided to try across the lake but I wanted to fish along the way, so we put our poles sticking out the side of the canoe like outriggers and trolled our way over there.

This was the ticket. We hadn't gone fifty yards and we both had a fish on. Two ten-to fifteen-pound fish at the same time required some doing in order to land both fish. We decided I would let mine stay out away from the canoe, while Valarie landed hers. Dad had brought two big dip nets, one short handle and the other long. We had the short one. Val scooped up her fish and got it on the stringer. Then she could manage the canoe while I landed mine; teamwork that's a necessity in a canoe.

I don't know how many fish we caught and released as we worked our way around the north end of the lake. Right at the end of the lake the mountains are on both sides and went straight up a dead end to the canyon. Val caught what had to be a twenty-pounder. We turned around and went back over the same spot and this time it was my turn. We spent the next several hours going back and forth over that hole. Almost every time one of us would catch a fish. We had our four for the day and it was barely two in the afternoon. So we headed back to see what Mom and Dad were doing at the other end of the lake.

Dad said he had kept one out of eight he had caught and was having the time of his life. Mom, on the other hand, hadn't caught a thing. She had just sat there all day with this cheap little old Zebco rod and reel Dad had for her to use.

The next day, the girls had had enough for a while, so Dad and I went down the lake to the hole Val and I had found the previous day. That morning we didn't miss a beat. Every time our lines passed through the hole we caught a fish. Two of this size fish on at the same time was just too much to deal with. So I finally put my pole up and just paddled the canoe, letting my Dad catch and release all day. By the end of the day he had his first three fingers taped up from where they were line burned, and he just kept going. I asked him a couple of times if he had enough and he'd said "No, one more pass over the hole," back and forth until almost dark.

I had done it; I wore him out doing what he loved most: fishing.

You're only allowed to keep two fish a day in Canada. We soon found it didn't take long to fill our ice chests with fish. The fish were Dollyvardin Trout, a landlocked salmon, they have to be one of the most beautiful fishes there are. If you do the math, four of us multiplied by our ten day trip we could have had forty of these fish.

What do you do when your camping ice chest is full to over-flowing? You load both ice chests into the land cruiser and headed back in to town. We had seen a place on our way through that would take your fresh fish and trade you smoked or canned equivalents. Now we had a couple of cases of cans and three boxes of smoked Salmon.

We ate fish sandwiches for lunch and baked fish campfire style for dinner. We all loved fish but you can only eat it for so long when a steak is in order. The town being not that far away, we all hopped in the land cruiser and ran back into town to do some shopping and take ourselves out to dinner at the local steak house. After six days of camping we all were ready for a shower. In Canada, they have pay showers like a car wash where you put in quarters for so much shower time. We found out what the expression "six bits dirty" really means.

The last two days were spent just lazing around, sorting out piles of stuff that would have to go back into the vehicles for the long trip home.

Val and I took the canoe for a spin just to get away from the folks for a minute. We just sat out there on the lake listening, watching a pair of osprey mating over the water. The surface of the lake was so still and mirror-like, it looked like there were four of them instead of two. What a place to ponder life's meaning. We were totally content with ourselves for having been able to share this trip with my parents and each other.

The last morning of our trip, Mom had gone the entire time and still hadn't caught a fish. Everything was loaded up but the canoes and poles. We went for our last outing on the lake. Val and I went off to the north end to take our last pictures of this beautiful paradise, while Mom and Dad were fishing near the camp.

You must understand how quiet it is up there, except for the screech of an occasional eagle, it's dead quiet. Voices will carry great distances across a still lake. All of a sudden we heard my Dad screaming at my Mom, do this, don't do that, hold this up, etc. Val and I paddled around the little point so we could see them.

There was Mom; hanging on to that little pole with both hands while something towed their canoe along behind it with what seemed like no difficultly at all. The fish pulled them out into the middle of the lake, turned around, and pulled them to the other side. We had never seen anything so comical. I thought my Dad was going to bust a gut; all I heard Mom say was "Don't yell at me". After fifteen minutes, the fish was exhausted, and Mom just reeled it up next to the canoe where Dad scooped it up in his giant net. It required two hands to get this fish into the boat.

This fish was forty-eight pounds and was at least twice the size of anything the rest of us had caught; this fish gave mom the bragging rights for the rest of her life. She made Dad mount that little ragged pole over the mantle to keep his version of the story at least close to correct.

I made a lot of trips with my parents as a child. Being a military family we moved and traveled extensively, but the trip home was undoubtedly one of the happiest I had the privilege to make with them. It was truly one of the high points in my life as well as theirs. We sang songs and played the Alphabet Sign Game which is how I learned to read, and Name the Capitals game. It was grand.

When we got back home, fishing took a back seat to snow skiing for the next few months, but spring was coming and so was the *Ultimate Fish Story*.

144   *The Ultimate Fish Story*

The Winter Storms

That winter, storms pounded the beaches with twenty-foot waves almost daily. The ocean roared day and night, for the whole month of January. The giant waves shook our house. They created enough salt mist in the air to carry a quarter-mile inland. We normally slept with the window open to hear and smell the surf and salt mist but not this winter. The house was buttoned up tight. The storm surge pushed huge piles of kelp and flotsam up on the beach that winter. In the twenty plus years that I lived there I had never seen that much debris piled on the beach. I mean, all the beaches from Monterey to San Francisco were covered four or five feet thick with kelp and driftwood.

Driving up the coast, we could see that most of the kelp beds we liked to fish in were gone, ripped away by the huge waves of the winter storms.

The fishing was really bad that spring and several outings brought back no fish at all. We'd been fishing in the kelp beds for three years now and never had we not caught at least a few fish per trip. We didn't make many more tries that spring or summer as we watched and waited for the kelp beds to slowly return. It would take several years for them to recover from this past winter's storms. Actually, it took five years for the kelp to re-grow, but it was never as thick as it had been and the fishing never seemed quite as good.

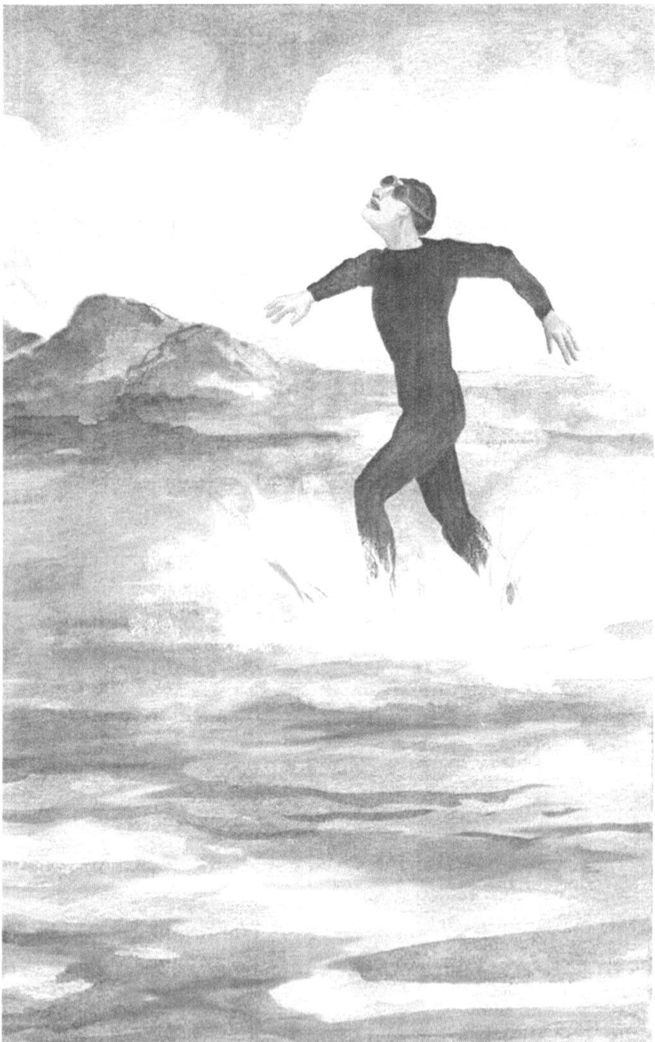

Walking on Water

Our adventures weren't limited to the canoe. We also had a communal twenty-foot day cruzer we had rebuilt, it matched our M.O. It was called *The Firefly*. It had two outboard motors, a fifty-five horse Mercury on one side and a twenty-horse Evinrude on the other, which ran most of the time. We fished with it when we couldn't use the canoe. But there were parking and launch fees, gas and oil, and all that just made it inconvenient.

But, we had an appetite for abalone, and Walter, our local crazy diver, would go get them. Walter wanted to go up to Ana Nuevo Island to go "abbin' ". He needed the boat because he couldn't get out through the surf to the rocks which lie beyond. He sold abalone to the local area restaurants and volunteered to pay me for the trip.

During the winter, Ana Nuevo Island just happens to be the Elephant Seal breading grounds for the entire California Coast. They calf in December and January and are there until the spring. All those little Baby Elephant Seals bring "The Great White Sharks" in droves. Nobody in their right mind would dive in that water when this is going on. Well, I didn't say he wasn't half crazy, O.K. maybe completely crazy.

On the way up, the huge twenty-foot swell was fairly smooth. I mean there wasn't any wind chop on top of the swell itself. The duration was also long, which made the ride like a gentle roller coaster. Up twenty feet, down twenty feet, from the bottom you can't see anything but sky and water. You looked around on top, yep; the shore is right where it belongs, then slid down into the next pit. In fact, that's what sailors and fishermen call conditions like these; they're called "rollers".

As we worked our way up along the coast, off to our side we were treated to a spectacular sight, a continuous rainbow, for miles above the beach. The spray off the huge waves, back lit by the sun, made a horizontal rainbow above the surf. Behind us, the crystal clear dark green ocean was split by the white "v" left by the boat as it slipped through the water over the rollers. It's no wonder people want to live there, there's so many beautiful things to see. You just had to get out and find them!

Both motors ran without missing a beat most of the way up there. The Evinrude was cutting in and out for the last three miles or so. So it slowed us down from thirty-five to twenty-five, but we got there.

Walter was showing me where he wanted to be dropped off. He said "Just hang around at the edge of these rocks; I'll swim back with the abalone." He was putting on his wet suit while we bobbed around in the backwash off the rocks. The onshore breeze carried the bleating calls of the Elephant Seals and their pups from a half a mile out on Christmas Island.

Finally ready, Walter bailed over the side. Hit the water and let out a God awful scream, as the cold water rushed into his wetsuit. I handed him the Tequila bottle for a final chug, and he was off. I watched him slowly swim fifty yards or so along the edge of the rocks and disappear under the water. He was towing an inner tube with a mesh net laced to it to put the abalone in when he found some.

He no more than went under when I watched a Great White Shark swim right next to the boat. I looked up and its head was close to the bow and I couldn't yet see its tail. This thing was twenty-five, maybe thirty feet long. It was as wide across its front as the *Firefly*; eight feet.

It turned and headed in Walter's direction. I could just see his next meal being Walter! There was a loud slap followed by a swirl of white foam and six feet of Shark tail ripped next to the rocks. I just knew Walter had become lunch. The shark rolled violently and slammed its head back into the rocks, turning the water into foam and sending some of it flying twenty feet into the air.

Still, Walter hadn't come up for air that I could see. He'd been down too long to hold his breath by my calculation. I was thinking "Oh my

God, I knew better than to do this, the damned shark's got him." The shark slammed into the rocks sideways again, trying to get in underneath them, churning the water white. Still no Walter, I guess the good thing was the water was still white and not red.

Then, out of the swirling water, Walter shot straight up. He seemed to stand on the water, motionless. He was blue, not white, against his black wetsuit. He stood there as an aberration of a famous person who walked on water. After what I thought was forever, Walter started moving towards the boat, still standing on the water. He wasn't moving but he was moving. Then he broke into a run, running on the water. I swear from what I saw it looked like he was walking on water. Somehow, Walter covered the thirty or forty feet and slammed into the side of the boat. I grabbed him, to make sure he wound up in the boat. The Shark scraped itself against the bottom of the boat making it quiver and list to one side. It made a strange sound come out of the cabin, almost like a viola. Walter's color was blue-white like the dead people in the morgue; he couldn't seem to talk. He just sat there, not even breathing. Finally he sucked in a great gasp of air, then another, and started choking up water while gasping for air.

    I never saw him again when his eyes were that big and blank. I handed him the Tequila bottle but he didn't seem to see it. I think he was coming back from the dead. I knew he was scared, as close to scared to death as you can get without staying dead. After a few more minutes he choked out "Holly Jesus, Did you see that? That thing had me pinned up under a ledge. I don't know what happened, man, I was scared shitless. I was looking straight into a mouth that could have swallowed me. He almost sucked me out of there, when he whipping his tail up against the ledge. And I'm pretty sure my ear drums are ruptured, 'cause they're ringing like crazy. I was holding onto the underside of rock for dear life." His hands were cut up from the sea anemones. "I passed out holding my breath. Next thing I know, you were grabbing me and hauling my ass in the boat." I had to tell him that he might have *heavenly* connections because he had just walked on water to get away from the shark.

We eased the boat over to pick up his float ring; he had managed to get three abalones before the shark found him. It was a drunken trip back, engines not running right, poke'n along, the boat just barely up on a plane. Walter didn't say much, he was nursing the tequila bottle. I figured he needed it all and probably some more when we got home.

That day Walter became the second person in the history of mankind to be able to walk on water. Years later, and after much discussion about the miracle, we never figured out exactly how it happened, other that it might have been Miraculous. Some of us think he was running on the shark's back. What do you think?

Walter never went abalone diving again and I can understand why. He said he had used up all the luck he would ever have that afternoon. I'm quite sure Walter thought it was well worth it.

You might wonder how in the world we could have a more fantastic story than this one. Well now, it's time to unfold *THE ULTIMATE FISH STORY*.

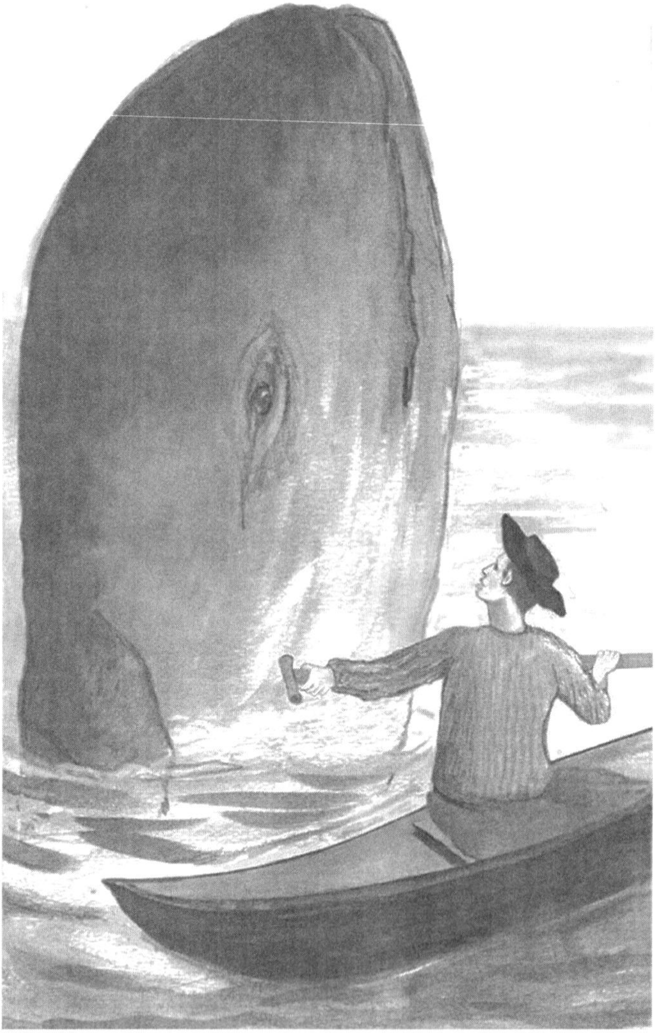

Craig's Trip and the Ultimate Fish Story

It was heading into fall and Craig had been bugging me about taking him out. He didn't care if we caught fish or not. He wanted to go for the trip, spending our afternoon drinking beer and watching the folks on the beach; a totally cool way to pass the day away. Finally, I agreed that we'd go on the next afternoon high tide. So I looked up the next favorable tide, in our ever handy tide chart for Monterey Bay. It was six days away

I know it sounds like whenever we wanted, we just jumped up and ran down to the beach, paddled our little canoe out, and went fishing; but that wasn't what happened. The tide had to be high and the surf had to be such that we could get through it and back again. We couldn't fish at all during the high tides.

The morning arrived and the fog was as dense as it could get. I mean, you couldn't see across the narrow street behind my house. One of those days you know the surf is close, but you just can't see it until you're on top of it. You don't really know how far away it is, either, just from the sound. Scary, if you're trying to find your way back to a harbor mouth. Some places along the beach, a jetty is sticking out a hundred yards or so, for the unwary. We knew the ocean was about two hundred feet outside my front door, but it was eerie not to be able to see it. Fog or not, it didn't happen that many times in the twenty-seven years that I lived there.

Craig showed up raring to go. So I had him load all the stuff. That was another reason for taking one of the kids along—pack animals. We got down to Capitola Beach and found the same pea soup fog. We didn't really care; we knew where we were going and how far it was. Still, heading out on the ocean is a unique adventure, every time you go.

That's why we went. You just never knew what might happen out there this time.

We carried the canoe down first and set it five feet or so from the water line. We started unloading our gear and piling it on the beach next to where we'd set the canoe to get it ready. The surf was calm, just enough so you could hear it. A gentle lisp and hiss in the sand, from six-inch waves. Everything was ready.

We set the canoe down at the water's edge. I pushed it out into a foot of water and Craig climbed in and got his paddle ready. One more little push-off and I got in while he started to paddle us out. By the time I started to paddle with him, we were half the distance of the pier out. I decided to just steer and let him do all the work.

Paddling alongside the pier we felt comfortable, knowing it was right there, looming up out of the fog, part visible, part faded into gray wisps. It looked like a setting for a scary movie or a London wharf. You know, when the bad guy jumps out and grabs you. Soon though, it slipped into the fog as did all other sounds, now just silence. The sound of the paddles in the water and the canoe slipping along; it was so quiet; we could almost hear each other breathe.

I told Craig to stop paddling and listen, to see what he would do with no reference as to direction. I asked him "What way would you go to get to the beach?" He had no idea but he took a guess and pointed out to sea. He was completely turned around already.

I started paddling slowly off in the direction I hoped would get us to the kelp bed and in ten minutes we were sitting at the edge of the kelp. We still couldn't see the beach which had to be less than fifty yards away. The water was crystal clear and we could follow the kelp all the way down to the rocks and sandy patches on the bottom. I said something to Craig about being able to see the bottom in twenty-five feet of ocean water. Generally, visibility in the area is about three to five feet and I remember he looked over the side and said "That's cool; with water this clear we should go abbin' later".

We moved a couple of times and only caught two small Gophers. We kept moving in closer to the beach, trying to make sure just exactly where we were. I was tying the canoe to the kelp, when I could see what looked to me like the bottom of the ocean moving. "Hey Craig," I said "Look over the side, man, I think the bottom is moving!"

All I heard was "Holy shit!". I grabbed my fishing pole and reeled it up as fast as I could, Craig did the same. We both kept looking over the side but the phenomenon was gone. "What the hell was that?" Craig said.

"I don't know man, but I think that's it over there". And he pointed to where the water just then exploded into foam and spray. Some of it was being thrown twenty feet in the air and it covered fifty square feet on the surface. It was loud, the sound of great amounts of water being moved violently back and forth. Then it stopped, a scary still, nothing but tiny bubbles. Craig was white as a ghost, he was holding onto the rails of the canoe with a death grip. He stuttered "What should we do?"

I said, "I don't think it matters what we do at this point, Craig."

Then it started thrashing around again in the kelp, but this time I recognized the blow of a whale, or at least I thought I did. We still hadn't seen anything but the effects of what it was doing. Then it stopped again, letting the bubbles come to the surface. From forty feet away the kelp started to part, something moving towards us under the water, something huge, coming straight at us. Then ten feet from the canoe it stopped, the kelp went back together.

Again nothing. Five or six seconds went by, then straight up out of the water and no more than six inches from the side of the canoe came a thirty-five-foot pilot whale which was probably fifteen feet around. I doubt if any of you have seen a pilot whale up close, but their eyes are six-or seven feet back from their nose on one this size. An eye that would be eight inches across and black as midnight.

This one was eye to eye with me. I mean not slightly close to being level but exactly eye to eye. I don't know what the focal length of a whale's eye is, but he must have had me up as close to him as he could; the proverbial bird's eye view. He was standing on his tail to hold himself up that high, and he stayed there for over two minutes. I didn't even blink, totally mesmerized by the whale's actions. I've had some really bizarre things happen in my life but this was the ultimate in fantastic. I wondered what in the hell this friendly giant could be thinking as we stared into each other's soul. There are things in this universe that some of us just know. There was a stillness and a trading between he and I; unexplainable in words. Finally, I jokingly said, "Nice to meet you, Brother Wizard". He seemed satisfied with my answer, for he slipped straight back into the sea.

His massive head went down so fast that when the void left behind filled with rushing water, a stream shot straight up. Well, almost straight up, it had enough of an angle that most of it landed on me.

Craig and I sat there speechless. The whale went back over to where he had been earlier and proceeded to thrash and pound around again even more violently than the first two times. Then, again, nothing but bubbles. I'm not easily impressed, but this tops the list of lifetime experiences and I was pretty sure it wasn't over yet.

Here he came pushing back through the kelp as he had done earlier. Craig and I grabbed the sides of the canoe. We just knew he was going to ram us, but at the last second he slipped underneath us. We both watched wide-eyed as this massive animal passed inches under the canoe.

Then with his tail, which had to be eight feet wide and five feet thick, he picked the canoe up out of the water. We were sitting on his tail out of the water. Then he dropped us back in the kelp as pretty as you please.

His gigantic tail came up again about six feet from the side of our canoe. It looked even bigger as he flipped it backward and covered us with a wall of water eight feet wide. He filled the canoe a quarter of the way up with this back wash, which made everything in the canoe float some.

Fifty feet away, as he headed out to sea, he blew a twenty-five-foot spout of water and air, sort of saying good-bye, I guess, and disappeared under the water.

Craig and I just sat there staring at each other. Finally I asked him "Did that really just happen, because I think I might have been having a flashback or something."

"No" he said, "it really happened. That whale looked you right square in the eye, man."

"I knew you were weird, but this, no one will believe me when I try to tell it; no one!"

He was right; I've since been a commercial salmon fisherman for several years, and a bush pilot in Canada and Alaska, places where chances to tell tall tales are in abundance, and no one I have ever met has had a better fish story than the last one in this series of fish stories. Hence the name *The Ultimate Fish Story*.

If having read this book, you feel that you have a story that comes close to this one, please see if you can get it to me.

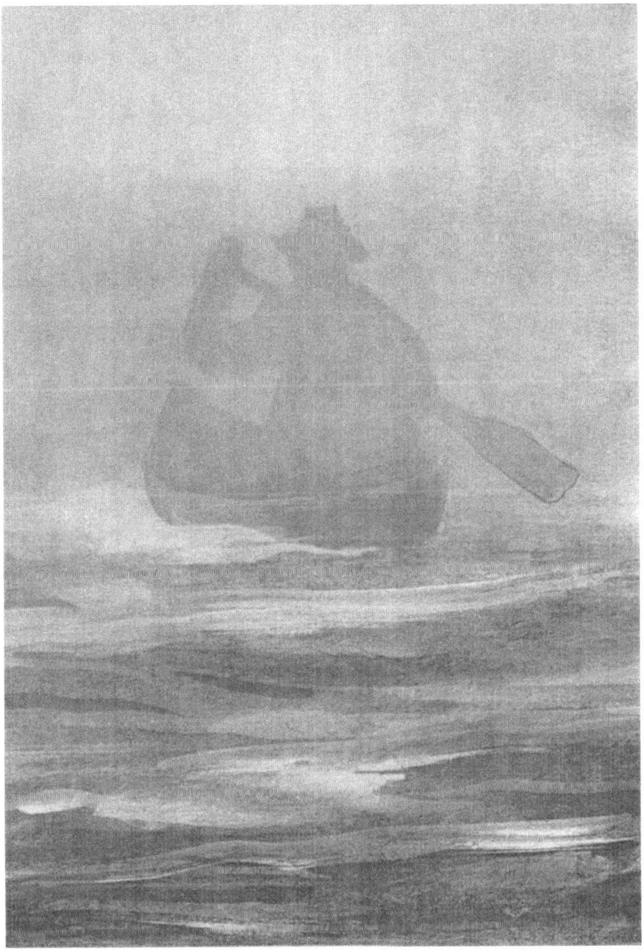

Harry Haney 171